THE IMPORTANCE OF BEING
PERCY

THE IMPORTANCE OF BEING

PERCY

The Bill Waddington Story

BILL WADDINGTON
WITH
STAFFORD HILDRED

BOXTREE

First published in the UK in 1992 by
Boxtree Limited
36 Tavistock Street
London WC2E 7PB

ISBN 1 85283 192 8
A catalogue record for this book is available from
the British Library.

Typeset by Litho Link Ltd., Welshpool, Powys, Wales
Printed and bound in Great Britain by
Cox & Wyman Ltd., Reading, Berkshire

Contents

FOREWORD

SOME OF THE CHARACTERS IN *Coronation Street* are just like themselves off screen. Others are as different as can be – you would hardly recognise them as the same people. I should know, as for every week over some twenty-five years I used to see them both performing in the Granada studios and off-stage in the canteen where I would often bump into a member of the Street cast at lunchtime. Now, I have to tell you that Bill Waddington falls exactly half-way between these two categories. He has all the good characteristics of Percy Sugden – his good humour, vigour and friendliness. He does not, however, share Percy's propensity to pompousness, prigishness and absolutely no one could call him a nosy parker. He is, in fact, one of the most popular members of the cast, always ready with a one-liner and the first person to consult if you are thinking of backing a horse. His knowledge of matters concerning the turf is phenomenal and I don't know whether he trained himself to study his lines quickly by developing his memory on racing form or whether it is his experience as an actor that allows him to reel off all manner of statistics about this year's crop of three-year-olds.

But seriously, a lot of Bill's character and personality is reflected in this wonderfully enjoyable book. And it is a remarkable story of success and achievement late in life, which, as one of the same vintage as Bill, I heartily applaud.

Denis Forman

THE IMPORTANCE OF BEING
PERCY

CHAPTER ONE

Coronation Street

THERE'S ONLY ONE PERCY SUDGEN! One Percy Sugden! One Percy Sugden! There's only one Percy Sugden!

I had just stepped on to the pitch at Old Trafford to make a prize presentation before the big Manchester 'derby' match between United and City when I heard 45,000 football fans chanting. Then I knew Percy had really arrived. That deafening roar of approval from the people of my home city warmed my heart and was yet another stirring tribute to Britain's number one television show.

To me Coronation Street is more than just a programme. It's a wonderful way of life, a happy family, and the icing on the cake of a long and rewarding showbusiness career.

I was two years over the state retirement age, living alone and still quietly grieving the loss of

Lilian, my beloved wife of thirty-two years, when Percy came into my world.

Still blessed with far too much energy to contemplate putting my feet up, I had been sitting alone and pouring out my heart to my late wife, explaining that what I really needed was a new challenge, a demanding job, something to really get my teeth into.

It was FA Cup Final Day, 1983. Manchester United had just been held to an exciting draw by Brighton and Hove Albion. With my thoughts still racing about the match I received a telephone call.

Would I be prepared to join the regular cast of Coronation Street as Percy Sugden, the new caretaker of the community centre? He was to be cantankerous and grumpy; did I think I could play a miserable man after a long career as a comedian and funster?

Would I? Just you try and stop me. My mind raced back to my conversation with Lilian. I knew I would go into Coronation Street if it meant reading out the telephone book every night. I was absolutely elated.

In the nine years since that happy day Percy
Sugden has changed my life. I'm seventy-six
now and the grouchy old blighter still puts a
spring in my every step.

I'm having a ball playing Percy. Certainly, I
was a little cautious at first. Having been a
joker for all those years I wasn't totally confident in the early days that I would be able to
capture the character.

As a comedian I always wanted to be liked;
the hardest part of being Percy was that I was
frightened to death I would be hated. But I
realise now that he is loved. On the surface he
is rude and interfering, certainly, but he is also
honest. His strength is his honesty. If he is
played dead straight and with conviction it
becomes funny.

With the skill of the writing and the strength
of the team to rely on, I realised that, delivered
deadpan, Percy's lines can be just as funny as
the straightforward comedy that has been my
life.

I was thrust on stage as a wartime comedian
and I had been wise-cracking my way round

the country ever since. With a Royal Variety Performance before the Queen and box office successes up and down the country, I knew I had already had more than my share of magical moments.

Playing Percy has given me a great deal to chuckle about, for Coronation Street is just as much fun to make as it is to watch as a viewer.

I was delighted when Percy landed the job of school crossing patrol warden. It gave the old soldier the chance to get back into uniform. But I wasn't quite so happy when some lewd-minded joker in the cast decided to deface my sign. When I turned up for my first scene as a warden, the whole cast just looked at me and burst out laughing.

I stood there holding my sign, which said 'STOP CHILDREN' in huge letters, and they all roared with laughter at me. I looked down first to see if my flies were undone.

Then I looked up, to see a condom neatly attached to my sign. Somebody thought that was the best way of stopping children and I was happy to join in on the joke. I never did find out who did it.

One of our favourite ways of relaxing in between scenes is going for a swim in the private baths near the studios. Bryan Mosley, Bill Tarmey, Chris Quinten (who played the late Brian Tilsley) and I were regular swimming pals and we always enjoyed a joke. But we just about caused a riot when Bryan Mosley showed off his fancy new swimming shorts.

Bryan, who plays Alf Roberts the shopkeeper, really likes a bargain in real life too, and when he was in America he bought a pair of stylish new swimming trunks for four dollars, priced down from eighteen.

We soon found out why they had been reduced so drastically. As soon as he jumped into the water they turned instantly and completely transparent!

Heaven knows what the other swimmers thought. We all expected to read about 'Alf Roberts in nude swimming shocker' in the next day's papers.

Liz Dawn, who plays the dreaded Vera Duckworth, quickly became a special friend. I remember, after one of my early scenes as grumpy old Percy, she grabbed me and gave me a big hug and said, 'Ooh we've needed someone like you for ages.' That meant a lot to me. We were doing a rehearsal for some filming one day and just for a bit of fun I said, 'Lend me your wig.'

I quickly slipped it over my bald head, minus the cap of course, and went on in Vera's place. I got quite a few lines out before anybody realised what was going on. That wig is so famous nobody noticed it wasn't Vera.

Percy is always getting into scrapes. I think his worst moment came when he was knocked down by a car. It looked as though he had really bought it.

We had some real ambulance men in for the filming to make it look as authentic as possible. We were filming in public streets and I was supposed to be really badly injured. I was lying there flat out on the stretcher, trying to look as gravely ill as I could manage. Just as I was being carefully carried on to the ambulance by the genuine ambulance men, a little boy came rushing up and asked for my autograph.

I opened one eye and said,'Hop it, I'm dead.'

The only real problem I have with playing Percy is remembering all my lines. Percy pontificates so much he sometimes uses words I've never heard of. I've been known to reach for the dictionary to find out exactly what I am supposed to be going on about.

To make sure I won't forget the vital word I often write it on a beermat in the Rovers. Or even on my finger. If ever you see Percy gesticulating and waving his arms about you can bet your life I have got a key word written on my hand and I just need a glimpse of it.

We always have a laugh about my memory. Bill Tarmey's favourite trick is to switch beermats at the last minute to try to leave me speechless, but he has never quite managed it yet.

And when Les Dawson joined us briefly for part of the thirtieth anniversary celebrations he and his pal Roy Barraclough, who plays

Alec Gilroy so marvellously, managed to get a mention for my little helpers. As they walked through the Rovers, Les casually moved a beermat.

'Hey, be careful with that,' said Roy. 'That's Percy Sugden's script.'

When Alf Roberts had heart trouble Percy went to see him at home to cheer him up. Two particular words in my script were giving me some trouble so I took a broad piece of sticky tape, wrote the words clearly on it, very large, in ink and stuck them inside my cap.

They had to be quite large, as I wasn't wearing my glasses at the time; and of course, as Percy has manners, I had to take my cap off and rest it on my knees. So I knew I'd get a chance to look at it. As usual, with the confidence of having the words there if I needed them, I did not look down and got through the scene.

But afterwards the make-up man came up to tell me that I had two large words printed on my bald head. The heat of the lights had made me sweat and there they were. I had to have a peroxide clean-up and go back and do the scene again!

At Christmas Percy briefly had the job of playing Father Christmas at the Bettabuys Supermarket. He wasn't a great success. It got so hot in my grotto that my moustache kept falling off. At one point I got so annoyed about it I shouted, 'I'm fed up with this 'tache!' and it shot across the set.

The script has a little lad called Carlton coming in to see Father Christmas with a long list of what he wanted. When the scene was over Vinny, our prop man, said, 'Where did he get a name like Carlton?' I said, 'He must have been born in the back of a Vauxhall.'

Joining Coronation Street and helping to create a popular character out of crusty old Percy has been wonderful. When I arrived in the serial Jack Howarth was still very popular as Albert Tatlock, the First World War victim of the terrors of the trenches.

Percy and Albert would often find themselves sharing old soldiers' recollections, even though mine were from World War Two. Jack was a great help to me in my early days as a regular but sadly he was then nearing the end of his time in the Street.

It is an enormous move for any actor to join Coronation Street. However accomplished they are, the punishing schedule and terrific demands of producing three top quality episodes a week take some getting used to.

I received fantastic support, which was a great help to me, and I quickly understood why there is no individual star of the show. The show is the star.

Credit for its continued success should go in many directions. One week, early in my new role, I counted how many people made up important parts of the team and it came to around eighty. Not one of them could we really do without.

No wonder Sir Laurence Olivier, as he then was, wanted to sit silently as a tramp in the Rovers Return, just so he could say he had been in the Street.

No wonder the enchanting Princess Diana could not resist asking me if Phyllis Pearce would ever catch up with Percy. I answered, 'No, your Highness. Not if I can help it!' She roared with laughter.

My old friend from my variety days, Jill Summers, plays Phyllis and she does it brilliantly. A lot of fun comes from her endless pursuit of Percy. Wherever I go people, especially young children, take off that deliciously deep voice of hers and ask, 'Do you want a cup of tea, Percy?'

The partnership is so popular that we are in constant demand to make personal appearances. We travelled together right down from Manchester to Folkestone for one brief double act in a big night club, but it turned out to be a memorable trip for all the wrong reasons.

First, Jill hurt her leg. But, being the trouper she is, she insisted on fulfilling our engagement. Then we had a nightmare trip from London to the coast in a taxi whose headlights pointed permanently skywards. They were fine for picking out enemy bombers sneaking in over the English Channel but less useful for illuminating the road ahead.

Eventually we arrived and were immediately intrigued to find that we were being followed on the bill by a performing pig. I'm glad it was that way round in the event, because the poor creature was so alarmed by the experience it failed to dance as predicted and instead turned the stage into an indescribably smelly farmyard. Jill and I laughed our heads off from the wings.

People ask me if we all get on well together. We do. We simply have to. If we're doing up to sixty scenes a week the pace is so punishing you have to help each other. When Barbara Knox won her Best Actress award we all applauded long and loud. She could well win again, or this time it could be Thelma Barlow, who is marvellous as Mavis, or Sue Nicholls who is so good as Audrey Roberts.

All the other actors have become my friends but I must give a special mention to Bill Tarmey, or William as he now calls himself. I so admire the way he has worked his way up in life. He began as an asphalter in the building trade and got into showbusiness by singing in the clubs with his fine voice.

He managed to get small parts in various television shows before forcing his way in to Coronation Street as that terrific character Jack Duckworth. William had a heart by-pass operation three years ago and never once did I hear him complain. We love him, he's a great mate.

William Roache, who plays Ken Barlow, has become another very good friend to me and is most helpful to all of us. He is a kind, deep-thinking man always happy to help anyone with problems. The businessman of the pro-gramme, appropriately, is Johnny Briggs, our Mike Baldwin. He'll finish up in the million-aire bracket. He is a shrewd and likeable Londoner and a very good actor.

I really could go on and on about everybody but it would take another book to fit in all my thoughts on Coronation Street.

All the cast and the team behind the scenes

have my total respect. Even after nine years I still feel like a newcomer. I'm proud to be surrounded by so much talent, and I'm very confident that the younger members of the cast have what it takes to keep the show going on for a long time yet.

The former Poet Laureate, Sir John Betjeman, was a devoted fan. He said he was in heaven every time Coronation Street was shown and he let it be known that after he was gone he would love some cast members to be at his memorial service.

Barbara Knox, Bryan Mosley and myself had that honour and as we walked quietly in to Westminster Abbey, one of the sidesmen bustled over and asked for our autographs. Our characters and the show had such appeal that the crowds prevented us leaving by the front door – we hade to go out by the back door to avoid being mobbed.

Coronation Street reaches people in every walk of life. I went to Aldershot to visit the Army Catering Corps and the commanding officer told me that everything stops for the Street.

I was delighted when I learned that Percy had a military background, for although I was never a Desert Rat I did serve throughout the Second World War and I'm proud to have taken part in the Normandy Landings. The Normandy Veterans' Association badge I wear in the show is my own and I get letters from the many branches all over the country asking about it. I visit some of them and dearly wish I had time to get round them all. I went over with the Scots Guards as part of the Stars in Battledress to entertain the troops. I still get letters from old soldiers like myself asking incredulously, 'Are you the same Bill Waddington who entertained us on the beaches at Arromanches?' I'm proud to say I am.

Writer Harry Kershaw, who helped to create so many of the earlier Coronation Streets, gave Percy his own authentic memories of the war in the desert, which seem to strike a chord with many viewers. After Percy said, 'I made gravy under shellfire', I found that T-shirts printed with this immortal line were being worn by at least five different Percy Sugden Appreciation Societies. How marvellous!

Percy is honest, as honest as the day is long, and I feel it is heartening in this day and age that he has inspired all these Percy Sugden Appreciation Societies. The best part about meeting them is that ninety per cent of their members are girls aged between eighteen and twenty-two. Most of them are at university; they like Percy's frankness and they like his openness.

I have known the Beverley Sisters since my variety days. They have thee daughters who also sang in a group. When we did a show together at the old Manchester Playhouse, the young girls said they all like and respect Percy because they feel that if they were in trouble he is the one person they could go to for help.

He would do his damnedest to get them out of trouble. He is fearless. He has gone through the university of life in many ways; he has been through a war. And while much of life today makes him shake his head he believes in standing up for his principles. I am with him there, and there are one or two other things I have in common with Percy which arrived as coincidence. The writers didn't know it when they prepared my early scripts.

For instance, I volunteered for the forces in 1939 and inside six weeks, like Percy, I became a NCO cook. I come from a farming, butchering family from Oldham and I can cook. It is straightforward cookery, nothing fancy at all, but if I cook it you can eat it.

I also live alone now, and understand how he feels. Anyone like that who has been a man of the world, when they retire they want to go on being involved. Many times they go over the top and so does Percy, he gets involved in lots of things that are none of his business, but that's the fun of the man.

At all times he is entirely honest, very straight, that is the strength of the character. It is nine years since I started. I played four other characters, including being best man at Emily Bishop's marriage to the dreadful Mr Swain, before I became Percy, but none of them registered as he has done. I don't talk about them.

But I have had an amazing career that spans the change in showbusiness from variety to television. When I first came into the Street I was pulling back all the time. I didn't need to raise my voice to reach the back of the hall. (I never used microphones. They make you look as if you're sucking a lollipop.)

You have to believe what you're saying when you're acting. Although I've been in the business longer than anyone else in the programme, apart from Jill Summers and Betty Driver, who plays barmaid Betty Turpin, I still listen to advice from anyone, especially the good artists.

I was astounded by the public response when Percy lost his job as caretaker and the flat that went with it. After he was seen sitting alone in the park I was deluged with sympathy letters. It was an amazing reaction. A similar thing happened when I suffered a broken ankle. I fell over one of Phyllis' Golden Delicious apples, which are French, much to patriotic Percy's horror. I was overwhelmed by messages of sympathy, and the French Fruit

Growers sent me a free box full of apples and a T-shirt. I wrote back thanking them very much and saying in a few weeks' time I would be falling over a bottle of champagne!

Percy's plight always seems to tug at the heartstrings. When his landlady, Emily Bishop, was thinking of selling her house and moving off to Rhos-on-Sea I got lots of genuine offers of accommodation from concerned viewers. And Emily and Percy were even offered the jobs of steward and stewardess of a golf club at Rhos. Eileen Derbyshire, who plays Emily, is a special friend. It is great for me to have so many scenes with someone who is so thoughtful and stimulating to work with.

They told me just to play the part as I saw it when we began, but early on I wasn't entirely happy about how miserable Percy seemed to be. After I had been in the show about four months, however, the *Daily Mirror* did a readers' poll to discover the popularity of television stars from all over the world. I was astonished to find that they had me as the third most hated man on TV; there was JR from Dallas and Alexis from Dynasty and then Percy Sugden.

I told our producer at that time, Bill Podmore, and he said, 'Great. That means you must have arrived, because if you think about it, you're much better to be talked about than ignored.'

But I never get any abusive letters; I think the viewers must love to hate Percy. I have a much younger attitude than Percy, he's older than me.

When I got the job as school crossing patrol warden I put the outfit on and marched proudly about and said how marvellous it felt to be back in uniform. The head of traffic safety from Nottingham wrote to me with a list of mistakes I'd made and questioned my fitness to do the job.

We wrote back and said there was some poetic licence in a drama series. I said I had never been a school crossing patrol man before and hoped I never had to become one, but that I have to do what is written for me and I rely on the writers.

I said I would have to go and watch a patrol man at work, and added, 'Thank you for all your observations, and for putting your advice in such a clear way. But with respect to paragraph five, where you say I should have a medical, Percy Sugden will be twice as fit as you are when he's been dead a fortnight.'

People say to me, 'You're very very fit – how do you do it?' I say, 'Jogging.' Jogging? Yes. I never do it. You never see a jogger with a smile on his face, they're all killing themselves. You've only got so much mileage in your legs and your body and your mind, so why run yourself to death.

I look after myself, eat and drink sensibly. And I work hard and I think that's helped me through life. I do a lot for old folks. I feel very sorry for them; what worries me is that ninety per cent of them are women. I hate old people's homes, they're just God's waiting rooms; the people there seem to have lost all interest in life.

I feel very privileged to play Percy. He means such a lot to so many people. Three years ago

an old lady from Stockport wrote to me: 'Dear
Mr Sugden, Can you do anything about getting cheaper telephones for old people? We
depend on the telephone for keeping in touch
with our families. You can probably do something. Our MP is useless.' I am very fond of
Percy.

When people criticise Percy I just laugh and
say, 'What's up? I have to live with him.' When
I do after-dinner speeches as myself rather
than as Percy, just to show I am nearly human
I take a look around the room and say, 'Could
you wait one moment, ladies and gentlemen, I
want to make sure that there is no one here
with a blue rinse.'

I get the blame for most things in Coronation Street. You remember when Gail had her
baby – I got the blame for that, but I was too
proud to deny it.

The great thing about the Street is that it has
brought me into contact with so many marvellous characters. Margot Bryant, who played
Minnie Caldwell, was one of them. There was
a time when she was having a few problems

with her bank manager and he took her to lunch to sort it out. They went to a restaurant in Brighton, near where she lived, and a funeral party happened to be eating at the other side of the room.

The chief mourner came solemnly over for the inevitable autograph and said, 'I've just buried my wife.' Margot looked at him very firmly and said, 'Did anybody see you do it?'

I was walking along the front of Llandudno when a lad of about twelve came up to me with a middle-aged gentleman and a little lad of about six, who was his brother. The older boy said, 'Will you shake hands with my deaf uncle?'

I shook hands and then the lad said, 'Will you sign that?' and he handed me a tatty bit of paper. I said, 'I'll do better than that. Seeing as you know who I am I'll give you one of these.' And I handed him a signed colour photograph. I said to the smaller boy, 'Do you know who I am?' And he went blank. His brother said, 'It's Percy Sugden.' I said, 'It doesn't matter, I'll give you one anyway,' and walked on.

Fifty yards up the promenade the little lad catches me up and starts pulling at my jacket. I said, 'Hello, love.' He said, 'I've been thinking.' I said, 'That's good.' He said, 'I've had my photograph taken, and if you can tell me who I am I'll give you one of mine.'

I love Coronation Street; I like the recognition, the way the show gives me a chance to prove that I can still do a bit. I love the feeling of warmth that comes with the programme. It's almost as good as the money. It's given me a new lease of life. I have a nice home, but I can't imagine just sitting around doing nothing.

Now the studio tour is open, viewers can come and see the set for themselves. Thousands of people a week come to stand outside the Rovers and walk down the famous little road. I saw one woman walk from one end to the other. Then she stopped, took off her shoes, wrapped them in tissue paper and put them in a bag. She put on another pair she had brought. She said: 'Now I can say my shoes have walked down Coronation Street, I'll never wear them again.'

So many thoughts crowd into my head about the drama serial that has become such an important part of my life. The only people who annoy me are the ones who moan that it is not like real life. I think the reason Coronation Street is so successful is that it is an entertainment. It is not a documentary.

And it reaches so many people. My great love outside the Street is racehorses. I have bred them successfully for twenty years and I still have ten horses, which takes me to stables and racecourses round the country.

I am constantly amazed when top trainers rush to embrace me and affluent owners slap me on the back just as effusively as the ordinary punters who queue up to cry, 'Good on you, Percy'. Happily they all say, 'You make us laugh.' I think that is still my favourite remark. It makes me feel great.

The strength of the Street is the different characters. It wouldn't be interesting if everyone was nice and smiling and cheerful. Percy provided a bit of contrast. Percy is honest but he is misunderstood. Like anyone who lives alone, he wants to be involved with his neighbours, and what goes on outside the house.

It is a real challenge to portray an irritating nosy parker who has a heart of gold despite all his infuriating actions.

I think the appeal of his character was best summed up by a lady viewer I met in a restaurant. She was an attractive woman and I was aware that she had been watching me all night.

At last she had to say something. She came across and said, 'I hate you, I think you're marvellous.' I said, 'Thank you, that was a wonderful tribute.' I think I know just what she meant.

CHAPTER TWO

Early Days

I HAVE ALWAYS BEEN A NUISANCE, right from the start. I was born halfway through the First World War, and halfway through a Saturday lunchtime drinking session at my parents' pub, the Clarence Hotel, in Manchester Street, Oldham. My father was looking after the pub. He had just been discharged from the Army; he was invalided out of the Army Medical Corps. But that day he was more worried about keeping pace with the growing throng of weekend drinkers than about the latest grim news from the front.

The pub was quite busy and in between pulling pints my father apparently said to one of the barmaids, 'Where's Epsie?' That was my mother's name. 'She's upstairs having a baby,' was the rushed reply. 'This is a fine time to do something like that,' said my father. 'She ought to be downstairs helping me.'

Ever since then I've had a knack for popping up and getting myself noticed. And I was born with something that brought a lot of attention to the pub, a veil over my face. When I first arrived I had a caul, a thin membrane of skin, covering my face. It is a phenomenon much treasured by sailors because they say if you have one of these things you will never drown.

In those days this superstition was very strong and my mother was so proud of my veil it was kept on show in the pub. Eventually it vanished at the same time as one of our regular customers, a sailor, and we never saw him or it again. But to this day I have no fear of the sea because of the confidence it has given me that I will never drown.

My parents were both very, very hard working. My father was only half joking when he grumbled about my untimely arrival. And my mother was back behind the bar pulling pints that night.

My father was a lovely feller with a smashing

dry sense of humour that I think I have happily inherited. He worked as an undertaker as well as a joiner. They had to do everthing in those days. He was William Waddington, the same as me, and Mother always called him Will. She called me Billy; I think she thought I was a goat.

He was very popular, my old man, and a good father. They had twin daughters called Marie and Ida before me but they both died as babies. They caught the 'flu' epidemic at the start of the First War and died within a week of each other. My sister was born in 1915 and I followed her some fourteen months later on June 10, 1916. It's strange, but if the twins had lived I don't believe my sister and I would have been here. We were compensation for the tragedy.

My mother's name, Epsie, was a very unusual one. I never found out where it came from, never heard of anyone else called that. She was a remarkable woman – a successful businesswoman in the days when most women did not even get to look inside their husbands' pay packets. She ran a string of butcher's shops as well as the pub. Her maiden name was Hague, and Epsie Hague looked very compelling on a shop front.

She was orphaned when she was about eight or nine and my mother and her sister and a younger brother were taken on and brought up by their uncle, Joseph Hague. She took his name, but her real name was Needham. Joseph Hague was a wonderful character. He was a commanding figure in Oldham, a wholesale butcher who was worth a lot of money. He used to make money while other people were thinking about it, Joseph Hague. He taught my mother his trade so well that when she was still a young woman she knew every aspect of the butchering business.

My father's father was a brass finisher, in more ways than one. I mean that was his job, but he was a boozer as well. My maternal grandfather was the headmaster of a school in Preston.

The rich and successful Hague side of the family were just a little disappointed when my mother went and married a humble joiner. My mother's uncle thought she was wasting herself; she should have married a butcher, they would have made a good business. But they were very happy together and my father did learn how to be a butcher.

My sister Connie was very sickly as a young child but I was tough. I used to resent it, when we went to school, because they would give my sister a penny to spend at the sweet shop and give me an apple or a banana. And if she hadn't been very well, they'd give her tuppence, while I still had to have the fruit. I liked fruit, but I would have also liked to have been able to buy liquorice. I was the kind of youngster, who would have felt he was begging if he asked. My mother would say, 'You don't need the money. Connie is not very well.'

I think I got my love of entertaining people from my mother and my sense of humour from my father. My mother loved the theatre and when we were very young she loved to enter us for the fancy dress competitions at all the local carnivals. And we always won.

She had the costumes made. Once she dressed me as an old English clown; I had all these frills, and I wore a proper wig with real hair sticking out. Then she got a professional clown to come and make me up properly. Everything had to be done just right. I had a string of sausages round my neck. They were made of cloth, and stuffed with sawdust to look like real sausages. And my father made me a red hot poker that I've still got.

I went as lots of different people, as Felix the cat, Doodles the famous clown, and as the Scarlet Pimpernel, and modesty can't prevent me from recalling that I won every time.

I started school at four, as one did in those days. But I was expelled from my first school. I wasn't a bad lad, but I was a lad. I used to get into all sorts of scrapes. I suppose I must have been about five when they asked me to leave. I was a bit inattentive. My mother sent me to Miss Dronsfield's private school hoping it would bring out the best in me, but it seemed to bring out the worst.

I was just mischievous. Every time the teacher went out of the room I would get out of my seat, creep up to the front and wipe everything she had written off the board. And then she caught me at it and my parents realised I was becoming a bit of a pest, so they decided to take me away.

I was just full of fun. I wanted to make jokes all the time and to make other kids laugh. Next I went to a little parish church school which wasn't too far from home, and I liked that. I looked forward to going to that school. We used go to the tuck shop across the road and get enough sweets to last all day for a halfpenny. I remember we used to buy these little halfpenny sticks of rock. They were very thin, and if when you bit it it had a red mark down the middle, you could claim a piece of jelly that was on the counter. You would really think you'd got something then.

My sister always had to stand with me in prayers – in those days every school day started with prayers – and the whole school would sing a hymn. I would sing at the top of my voice, and she would have to be beside me to quieten me down when I started to get a bit carried away. I was a bit of a pest, I must admit.

But although I was often rather inattentive, if anything was really interesting I would listen carefully. I can clearly recall one day at school when we spent a whole afternoon learning proverbs and famous quotes, like 'people in glasshouses shouldn't throw stones', 'a rolling stone gathers no moss', and 'where there's a will there's a way'. I was fascinated. At the end of the afternoon the teacher said, 'Now, can any of you children tell me any of those proverbs we have discussed today?' I jumped up, which totally surprised her; she couldn't believe it. I stood up and very proudly said, 'Where there's a well there's a whale!'

She fell about with laughter. She thought that was a huge joke and the whole class laughed. After a moment I laughed with them. That was the first laugh I ever got. I decided there and then that I liked the experience and I've been laughing ever since.

Later, my teacher told my father what I'd come out with. My mother had a shop on Oldham market and she and my father were at the shop, laughing about it. They asked me, 'Why did you say that, about the well and the whale?' I said, 'Well, that's where the water comes from. It's the whale that's doing it. You know, squirting water into the well.'

That was my childish logic. But the important thing was that I had enjoyed the way that what I had said had made people laugh. It was a new experience for me and it took a while to sink in properly.

I could always handle myself quite well. I was quite strong as a boy and I knew how to box. If someone was having a bad time from the school bully I would say, give me a halfpenny and I'll sort him out. They used to pay up and I would go and get stuck into this kid and teach him a lesson. Just think, I was a prize-fighter at five! I remember one day I had about six pennies in my pocket and my mother said, 'Where did you get all this money?'

I explained and she warned me that if I

wasn't careful someone would give me a good hiding one day. I said, 'He'll have to be bigger than me if he does.'

The idea of performing seems to have always been kicking around somewhere in my head. I think the first time I got the chance was at Sunday school. I went to Evangelists' Sunday school in Henshaw Street in Oldham. We were taught to dance there, ballroom dancing. Of course I was much more interested in running and jumping on the stage and chasing round like kids do.

When I was about six, the Sunday school was putting a play on called *The Mistletoe Bough*, and my heart lifted when I found out that there was a jester part in it. But it fell again when they picked another lad for it. I was very upset. I used to go and watch all the rehearsals from the back of the hall, and when it came to the dress rehearsal this lad got stage fright. All of a sudden he couldn't speak a single word. I saw all the grown-ups looking at each other and saying, 'What on earth are we going to do now?'

A little voice piped up: 'I could do it.' At first they wouldn't take me seriously. They couldn't believe that I knew the words, but I went on and on about it so much that they agreed to give me a chance. I stepped forward and did it without any bother at all.

I remember I had to sing: 'Eye-tiddley eye-tie, fee fo fum. You called your jester, here I come.' I had heard it that often I couldn't forget it, and I got the part. They made me a wig up out of cotton wool to make me look older and I really began to enjoy myself. Every time I jumped round the room in my jester's outfit the wig would start falling apart all over the place.

That was the first time I ever went on stage. But even then I had confidence, I wasn't nervous. I've got a quick mind, I always had as a youngster, and I use it.

At home, Mother was keen for me to develop as many different talents as possible. This violin arrived and I started lessons and was instructed to practise my scales regularly on this wretched instrument. I used to have to go to the bedroom, well out of earshot of my father. Fortunately at that time we had rather a large house. My only companion was this lovable Airedale dog, Twig, who used to sit there with me. I don't think he enjoyed the music much, but he liked being with me.

I could never be bothered to take the practising seriously. I just used to put the violin on the bed and have the bow in my hand, just pulling it backwards and forwards while reading the *Boy's Own Paper*. It sounded just as good as trying to play it properly. But one day my mother came in and caught me. I knew the dog wouldn't tell anybody, but I probably should have let him play; it wouldn't have sounded any worse.

When I was still fairly young my mother was so busy looking after her business and my sickly sister that she fostered me out and I only saw her at weekends. I stayed with a smashing couple called Mr and Mrs Robinson. They had a daughter of their own, but they took to me as if I was really theirs. I was very happy indeed with them.

They only had a small terrace house but it was always nippin' clean. They made sure I went to Sunday school every week, and when I came back they used to let me go into the kitchen and play on the slop stone.

A slop stone was a huge piece of stone that had been hewn so it could act as a drain with a basin on top. It would be about two inches deep. I used to put a piece of rag in the hole as a plug, and they would let me sail my little boat all Sunday afternoon. I used to spend hours happily doing that on my own because they were sleeping on a Sunday.

I can never remember being unhappy as a child. I had lots of fun. All the people I can remember from those days were real characters, who had time for a cheeky youngster. One of my favourites was Mr Lummox the baker. When I was just three, I used to climb over his big backyard wall and shout, 'Are you there, Lummox?' He used to give me little cakes over the wall. I will never forget the marvellous smells that used to waft out of that bakery.

My mother was quite a woman. It was out of

the ordinary for women to do any job then, and to run a successful business really set her apart. There was only one other woman butcher that I knew of, a Mrs Jordan, and funnily enough when I joined the Army I met her nephew, Dougie Jordan; but that is getting too far ahead of myself.

Yet my mother wasn't always working. She loved entertaining and whenever we had company I used to sing 'Moonlight and Roses' with her as a duet, even when I was quite a small kid. My sister would accompany us on the piano. Nowadays, whenever I hear that song a vision of my mother appears in front of me.

Our family was always moving. My mother should have been a gypsy. We had a shop, and we would live over the shop for a while, and then she would say, 'We're not stopping here.'

You could rent decent houses in those days for about twelve shillings a week. If you went up to fifteen you got a right belting place; for that much you could even have running water. One day, when I was leaving for school, Mother said, 'Right, when you come home for your dinner you come to 129 Horsedge Street, because that's where we are moving to.'

When I arrived at the new address my mother had got my food ready, because she believed in feeding me properly. But she stopped the fellows bringing the furniture in so I knew something was up. She told me, 'When you come home for your tea, come to 188 Ratcliff Street, because we don't like it here. We are moving again this afternoon.' So we moved twice in one day. She loved to move around all over the place, which meant that I kept going to loads of different schools, all around Oldham.

I found myself at the Freehold School in Werneth following one of our many house moves and I liked Miss Clegg, my new teacher, very much. She helped me learn how to concentrate, because I had been a bit of a lad, as I've explained. She was the person who coaxed me through five scholarships.

Miss Clegg never chastised me at all for being inattentive. She would talk to me and reason with me. I got to know her very well and

I got to pass all my exams thanks to her. She really got through to me. When I heard she was getting married, I wanted to take her a wedding present. I decided to take her one of the brass ornaments off our mantelpiece.

My mother was not too enthusiastic about this idea and we had a terrible argument about this ornament. She refused to hand it over. I wrapped it up and hid it. My mother found it and put it back where it should be, but in the end she let me take it.

I just liked Miss Clegg so much. I felt she was doing something for me. In the end I sat for my scholarships and passed them all. My father came down and said, 'Who have you been sitting next to?' But he knew I wasn't thick. I was just inattentive. If I set my mind to do a thing I could do it. And I could always rise to the occasion; I would steel myself and do it.

My swimming teacher was called Mr Pickles; I always remember his name because he got married to a lady called Miss Onions, so you couldn't forget that: Pickled Onions. It sounds like a gag but it's the honest truth.

I suppose I always had it in me to want to write comedy. I was just thirteen years old when I got a bit sweet on a girl called Gladys – until the day she had her lovely long hair cut and I saw the dirty neck she had obviously scarcely ever washed. I was so disillusioned I went home that night and wrote a poem about it:

> Oh Gladys I liked you till one night
>   when homebound,
> I saw your whole neck as you turned
>   round,
> I said to my friend,
> This sure is the end,
> And left you standing behind.
>
> Oh Gladys your neck is a dirty old wreck,
> And something is wanted to clean it,
> Pan shine and soap,
> May have a hope,
> But emery's the stuff and you need it.

Can you imagine that coming out of a thirteen-year-old lad? It was a cheek really. I met her years later when I was working as a traveller and she was still a nice girl. But she wasn't for me. Not with that dirty neck.

When I was still thirteen I had a bit of a set-back when I was struck down with rheumatic fever. God bless my mother's memory, she really looked after me. She was so very careful about what I was getting to eat, and she really cared for me and nursed me back to health. At that age the illness can be very dangerous. I was so ill I couldn't even bear the noise of anyone walking across the bedroom floor.

My mother said, 'Don't worry, I'll get you right.' She was a damn good cook. The doctor had instructed her that I was not to be given beef, so she fed me up on lamb and lamb soup and all sort of things like that. I was out of bed in ten days, which is unheard of. And the fact that I'm going strong at seventy-six suggests to me that she must have done a lot of the right things. They say rheumatic fever can affect your heart or send you bald. Well, my heart's all right. I'm bald, of course, but so was my father. I don't think the illness had anything to do with it.

My best pal at school was a lad called George Swift, but I had a lot of different friends because I kept changing schools so often. I went to one called Waterloo Street School. It was an old Victorian type of place and across the road there was a little cake shop. Every day when I was leaving the house I would ask my mother, 'Can I have a penny rice pudding for my dinner?'

My mother used to give me sandwiches for my lunch, then I would go across the road to the cake shop for something to go with it. My favourite was the penny rice pudding. One of my father's sisters, Auntie Ruth, lived round the corner from this school. She had eight or nine children, and the youngest, Walter, was a little baby then. I used to go back to their house with my rice pudding and he would stand there crying till I gave him some. So I took to going down a back alley and eating it somewhere else, and pretending I hadn't had one that day, because I was fed up of this kid pinching half my pudding.

I was a lad, but I was quite well behaved. I always felt full of life, very energetic. I won my high school high jump championship. I was tug-of-war captain. I finished up at Hollins High School.

And I was always good with my hands. I could make things. When I was very young I wove a lovely little mat with wool. We kept it for a long time in our house. I suppose because my father was a joiner and builder, I could do woodwork. I used to get the school prize for woodwork. I made a model of a ship, the *Santa Maria*, from a drawing, and I was really upset when the teacher wouldn't let me take it home.

I used to get into trouble by helping other lads who couldn't do a dovetail. The teacher didn't like this and got suspicious of me. Then one day he threw a wooden mallet right across the room at me and it just missed me. I picked it up and threw it back and I hit him. He never attempted to do anything like that again to me because I retaliated. The mallet hit him on the shoulder, because he moved a bit sharpish. If he hadn't done it would have brained him. He used to let us take our best dovetails and tenon joints home with us, but he wouldn't let me take this ship, and I was so upset about this that in the last fortnight I was at that school I did nothing else but make another one.

When I was ten I became a choirboy at Oldham Parish Church. I would sing, but the main reason I joined the choir was because in those days the choirboys wore Eton suits, long grey trousers, Eton jackets, toppers, a tall white collar and a bow. I liked the look of that outfit, so I joined the choir.

The other choirboys called me Paddy, because they found out early on that I had a temper. In those days they had a rather chilling initiation ceremony. I discovered this when they carried me out of the church and across the great big cemetery surrounding the building to a big tank where people could get water for the flowers they had brought to put on the graves.

I really did not fancy getting my immaculate new rig-out wet, and when I realised they intended to initiate me by dipping me in the tank I went a bit wild. I fought and struggled as hard as I could, and I'm proud to record that I got three of them in with me. I bashed two more of them quite severely. And I was supposed to be an angelic little choirboy. So I was given the nickname Paddy, for temper. I didn't mind that much, I did have a temper. If they left me alone I didn't bother anyone, but start messing me about and I got stuck in.

In the end I got expelled from the choir for pinching a couple of bananas from one of the Harvest Festival displays. They went mysteriously missing and as I was standing there with a mouthful of banana I was suspect number one. So they got rid of me.

Later, at Hollins High School, I joined the Scout troop. I had always fancied playing the bugle, and the Scouts gave me the chance to try it. I would go into a field near our house on a Sunday afternoon to practise. My father always liked to have a rest on Sunday afternoon after a lunchtime drink; he would shout at me to go further away and blow.

But I was better with the bugle than I had been with the violin and I thought eventually, after a lot of ear-bashing for the neighbours, I was quite proficient. I became a member of the bugle band for the Hollins Scout troop. We had a good bandmaster and he used to write lots of tunes for us to play. But I always had to be different. I've been like that all my life. We would play a tune and I would always have to finish it off with a twiddly bit at the end. It used to drive our bandmaster mad.

The great event of the bugling year was the band competition at Belle Vue, Manchester, where a silver bugle was the big prize for the best band. I was just as nervous and keyed up as the other lads as we arrived for the contest. And I was a little puzzled when, just before we started our routine, this little bandmaster came up to me and said, 'Hey, Bill, give me your mouthpiece.' I give it to him and he handed me another and said, 'Put this one in.'

I looked at my new mouthpiece and it was

solid metal. There was no hole in it. So I spent the afternoon blowing like billy oh and getting nowhere. My cheeks ached for about three weeks. But the bandmaster knew what he was doing. We won the silver bugle without anyone hearing a sound from me; and we wouldn't have done if I had been playing. I'd have put a twiddly bit on the end and spoiled it for everyone. I think I learned a little bit of acting that day, though I didn't know it. I went round blowing for all I was worth in case anyone guessed my mouthpiece hadn't a hole.

The Boy Scouts went to a place called Bare just outside Morecambe on a camping holiday. We all had to pay £3.10.0 for our week's holiday. There were some older Scouts there, Rovers they called them, and they were trying to take the mickey out of us younger lot. I was sitting there peeling potatoes when all of a sudden I felt a crack across the head, bang.

One of these berks had thrown a big meat bone from the other side of the camp and hit me. I pretended I was knocked out; I just lay there for a while and heard them talking, saying things like, 'You could have killed him.' I remembered their voices. I never let on; I pretended to come round, and I had a bloody great bump on my head big enough to put a bra on. I just bided my time for a few days, and still didn't let on I knew who it was. I found out that the lad who threw the ball smoked, and I went and asked him for a cigarette for the Scoutmaster. When he went to get it I noticed where he hid his packet and later when they went out I got his cigarettes and threw them in a bucket of water outside their tent. I always get my own back.

When I was quite a young kid I used to take the orders from my mother's butcher's shop. I had to cycle round and get through the orders before I could go off and play football. By the time I got to the match I was knackered. It took what was left of my energy to play and I was dropped because of that, because I was over-tired.

They used to have school inspectors walking about in those days, and one of their jobs was to check that children weren't carrying too much weight in their baskets. They would take your basket off you and weigh it. If it was too heavy then your family were in trouble. I remember having to dodge round a corner and take out the biggest parcel of meat and hide it under my jacket until the inspector had gone. I didn't want to get my mother and father in trouble. I used to save up the pennies I got for delivering; I was always one to make a little bit of money as a kid.

I had started making money as a prize fighter but that seemed a bit too painful for a career so I turned to butchering. I started by delivering the orders, then when I was older my mother would get me up on a Sunday morning, when we lived above the shop, and send me down to clean all the bones. I would get every tiny bit of beef or fat off them. I'd stand at the block and scrape them until they were like marble, and all that waste was then made into sausage. I suppose I was fourteen or fifteen by then.

My mother taught me very well. I could cut a lamb up by the time I was ten. I could bone

a shoulder of beef out then as well. I was
brought up to do it, and I was quite competent.
In those days you could buy a leg of English
lamb for three and sixpence, and a shoulder of
lamb for half a crown. You could buy fillet
steak for one and a penny a pound (just under
6p in today's money); shin of beef was sixpence a pound.

Young couples used to come in the shop,
they might have been earning only three
pounds a week between them, and my mother
would take great care to advise them how to
make their money stretch as far as possible. I
would stand in the background and listen.
They might say, 'We've only got one and sixpence to spend. What should we do, Mrs
Hague?'

She'd say things like, 'We've got some lovely
brisket this week. It's only sixpence a pound. If
you cook it slowly and press it you'll get three
good substantial meals off that.' I listened to
my mother's advice, which was always being
sought, and I learned that way. I could make a
Lancashire hotpot before I was twelve.

I was rather strictly brought up; my mother kept me on a very even keel. She was very busy looking after the pub and the butcher's shops, of course, but she always found time to keep a sharp eye on me. If I went to the pictures she always wanted to know who I was going with, and she had no time for girls. Once, when I said I was taking a nice girl I had met called Annie, she said, 'Oh, you have no time for girls,' and she wouldn't let me take her. She was very strict but she taught me such a lot that I am very grateful to her. She taught me how to cook, how to clean, how to wash, how to iron – how to look after myself in every way.

My school studies suffered a little bit because of my love of comedy and making people laugh. I managed to get to a grammar school, but on my last report the form master wrote: 'Your son is clown for the class. More attention would be very very useful.' He didn't really change my mind, though. Fun is very very necessary.

I left school at fourteen. I was so bent on respecting both my mother and my father, and

I wanted to prove to my mother that I could do things. I was given the job of looking after one of the butcher's shops on a Saturday afternoon. It was one of four new shops in a suburb of Oldham called Hollins and I used to get the old ladies coming in late on after everybody else had gone.

I used humour even then. I would say, 'Hello, love. Do you want a leg of liver or shoulder of kidneys?' Meat was relatively cheap in those days, and often I would give them half a breast of lamb on the side. They would always buy something from me so I built up a terrific trade.

Although it might not sound like a lot of money now, we used to take about £11 just on the Saturday afternoon, and that was very good going indeed. In those days you had a decent butcher's shop if you took £30 a week. There were four shops in the parade and I used to go along them and change all my pounds into ten-shilling notes to try to impress my mother, because it looked more when you lined it all up on the kitchen table for when she got back. And it worked. She was very proud of me. I would listen for them to come in and if she said to my dad, 'Well, he's not done so bad,' it used to give me a real kick. I would keep awake to listen.

One of my regular trips in those days was to the Manchester Abattoirs which were in Water Street, Salford. As a young lad I used to get up at three or four in the morning three days a week to fetch beef and lamb for the shops. That was the first real job of my life and it was literally just a stone's throw away from the Granada studios where, sixty-odd years later, I am now working on what is likely to be my last job.

I also looked after the lock-up shop and learned to make my own food, till my father found out I was cooking half a shoulder of English lamb for my lunch. He put a notice on the door warning me that one man killed himself through over-eating. I could eat, but I could also work hard.

I always wanted approval from my mum. I made a mistake one day, though, and my mother taught me a lesson. There was a girl, and a very attractive girl at that, who lived about four doors down from this shop. She was on the stage as a chorus girl. She was called Kathleen Edwards, I'll never forget her name. I was growing up a bit now, she was a nice girl and I talked to her. She came into the shop one Saturday and unusually she was not working that night. I plucked up my courage and asked her to come with me to the pictures. To my delight she said she'd come.

Now I had never been to the pictures on a Saturday night before. Normally I was too knackered. After working all day from six in the morning I always had the shop to scrub out after we closed. My mother insisted everything had to be spotless, and she had taught me how to do it. But that day I thought, I'll do the counters and windows quickly and then I'll long-mop the floor. I'll get plenty of soda crystals – to get rid of the grease, you see. I did this to hurry the job up and give myself time to go to the pictures.

When I came home I didn't switch the shop

lights on, and the next morning about seven o'clock my mother was standing by the side of my bed in her dressing gown. She just pulled my ear which yanked me quickly out of dreamland and said, 'I've got something to show you.'

I meekly followed her downstairs in my pyjamas and into the shop. She said, 'Would you please take a good long look at this shop floor.' I was wide awake by then and shocked by what I saw. It looked for all the world as if it has been whitewashed. In my hurry I'd overdone it with the soda and there were great white marks halfway up the skirting boards which were very definitely not allowed.

She said, 'Now then, that's not right, is it? You've long-mopped it instead of scrubbing it properly, haven't you? All right, you can sort it out, and when you've done it properly you can have your breakfast.' That turned out to be at half past two in the afternoon because I had to do it about five times to get all this damn stuff off. I still wonder whether Kathleen Edwards was worth all that grief.

I thought that was the end of the matter, but it wasn't. The following Saturday, she said, 'You're not looking after the shop this afternoon. I'm bringing Jack down from the stall in the market. I want you to go round the other shops and show the lads how to scrub floors.' So I can scrub floors with anybody even to this day. But that was the discipline in my life. I used to think she was a very hard taskmaster, but by God today I thank her, now I live alone I can do anything for myself.

My mother was a very strong lady. She taught me all the domestic skills – I learned a lot. With ironing, I started on the handkerchiefs and slowly moved on to shirts. My mother used to laugh a lot but only rarely did she let me see it. And she used to boast, 'Whichever girl marries my son, she'll have a proper husband. He can do anything, and if she can do it herself he'll join in with her.'

When I was fifteen my mother said to me, 'Why don't you go and get yourself a job with somebody else?' I was puzzled by this; I was getting on well, working for her and my father, but she explained that she wanted me to find out how other people did things. She said, 'Go somewhere not too far away, but don't tell them who you are. Your name is Waddington so they won't connect you with me. Go and get yourself a job.'

I went to the Argenta Meat Company in Tibb Street, Manchester, a big shop it was. I was the order boy and I got a surprise when I quickly realised I was more competent than half the fellows they had working in the shop. One day I said to the manager, 'Can I bone that shoulder?' He said, 'Do you think you can?' I said, 'Aye.'

I did it and he looked surprised. 'That's very good,' he said, 'you've done that before.' I told him that I had worked for a butcher in Old-ham, and that improved my job a lot. I started getting better jobs, boning shoulders and cutting up and preparing meat. He got very friendly with me and he said, 'You know something about this job, don't you?'

But gradually I grew to hate cutting up meat, and I still hate it. Meat was a commodity;

I never used to think it had once been an animal. I was a great animal lover even then. I could only do the job if I forgot about the animal.

When I'd been with the company for a while, the manager came and asked me if I could chase up an unpaid bill. He just wanted some money paid off the £18 which was owing. It was owed by an hotel and we were still taking them meat but they were not paying. The manager said, 'I don't care how long it takes you, but try to get some money if you can.'

I had to think about this one. I had never fancied myself as a debt collector. So I went round and said to this bloke, 'Here is your bill. My gaffer says I have got to sit here until it's paid. If I go back to the shop without your money I will get the sack.' He said, 'You had better sit there for a bit.' I sat down, as much in the way as I could manage, for half an hour, and then I heard him saying to someone, 'You had better give us some money to pay this lad otherwise he's going to be here all night.'

They gave me the money, paid up in full. I

went back to my shop with the whole lot and my boss just couldn't believe it. He wanted to know how I'd done it so I told him. And after that I got the job of collecting debts. Just because I had the cheek to do it. A bright-faced young lad who looked like losing his job seemed to work wonders on bad payers.

My enterprise must have had an effect for they moved me to be assistant to the manager of their branch in Oldham, not far from my mother's – they still didn't know who I was. It had a huge great window, twenty feet by ten, a very awkward window to dress. And it was a very unsuccessful shop for some reason; it just did not sell a lot of meat.

I was not taking round the orders any more, I had been promoted. I got a rise every week I was with that firm. Every single week I was there I got a two-shilling rise. The area manager used to walk round feeling under the counter to see if there were any teardrops underneath, but I had been brought up properly. I said, 'You're wasting your time doing that, sir, it's been properly cleaned.'

There was a big competition organised by
New Zealand Lamb for the best display of their
products and we were saddled with this huge
window to dress up. The manager said, 'We
don't have a chance with this great window. We
only sell three lambs a week, they will look daft
in the window.' I said, 'I tell you what. One leg
of lamb won't look daft.' He couldn't understand what I meant, but I just asked him to
leave it to me because I had an idea. I think he
was pleased to find someone else to take on
the job.

I went off to a second-hand shop and
bought a great big old picture frame for half a
crown. It was filthy. I took it home and
scrubbed it and it came up beautifully. I
bought some gold paint from Woolworth's
and painted it up. I draped the back of the
frame with ferns, and I put one solitary leg of
lamb on a silver server, and lit it up with a
60 watt bulb. That was the only piece of meat
in the window. My slogan was 'A perfect picture from your favourite company. Buy New
Zealand lamb,' and we won the competition.

We never went short of anything as a family. When I was eighteen I had the thrill of my life when my father bought me a car for my birthday. It cost £7.10.0 shillings, a Morris Oxford, a drop-head two-seater with a dickey seat in the back. I thought the world of that car. My father took me to this piece of open land and told me to drive around and learn how to stop. He said that was much more important than learning to make it go. And I used to drive up and down the little back alley beside the butcher's shop all day until I mastered it.

Then came the time for me to take my test – there were learner drivers then, I know it's a long time ago. I can remember going down for my test because it was down Lamb Lane – that sticks in your mind if you're a butcher. That was in Failsworth, by the Rialto Cinema. I was told to meet the examiner there.

I drove cheerfully up in my pride and joy, with nobody with me. The examiner said, 'Where's your driver?' I said, 'What driver?' I tried to say I didn't need one; with the un-shakeable confidence of youth I was sure I was going to pass my test.

'Well, all right,' he said grudgingly. 'Let's get on with it.' We drove around for about five or six minutes and he said, 'That's enough. You've passed. But you should have had a driver with you.'

In fact I had starting driving when I was about twelve. My father used to get me to put the car in the garage. It was a great big open tourer and I used to have to stand up to see where I was going. He used to laugh and shout, 'Don't go through the back whatever you do.'

That first £7.10.0 shilling car was marvellous. It was maroon, and the paint had very bad pigmentation marks. It looked like chocolate that had been left in the shop window with the sun on it. I didn't want it to look like that, because I always like things to look their best if they're mine. So I got some paint remover and scraped all this paint off. They were coach painted not sprayed in those days, and I painted it all with black lead paint. It looked absolutely smashing.

I was so proud of it, and off I went for a drive. While I was out it started raining and by the time I got back I looked like a black-and-white minstrel. This black lead paint had washed all over me; I was filthy. The following morning I went down to see my car and it was red rusty, because there was no protection in those days. So I had to go back to Woolworth's and buy another tin of Valspar and paint it again. It cost me another half a crown.

The biggest mistake I made was to lend it to a bloke to go Blackpool for the day. I told him he would be responsible for any damage and let him have it for £3 for the day. Inside half an hour he was towed back. He had smashed it into a wall. It cost him £25 to fix, and with his £3 it cost him £28. I was really upset. I never felt the same about that car.

I decided to look for another one, and I came across a lovely Austin 12, a sit-up-and-beg type with running boards, all-aluminium body and a rebored engine. I got it for £35. I took my mother and father down to see her younger brother, who ran a pub at Aston

Clinton down near Aylesbury. To get to this pub you had to go down a long lane and over this little hump-back bridge called World's End. The road just finished by the canal.

Ever the gentleman, while we were visiting I offered to take my very attractive cousin and her friend to this Catholic church in Aylesbury. On the way back I thought, I'll just have a bit of a run at that bridge and see what happens. I hit it flat out with engine screaming. We shot into the air and I looked down and there were three fellers with pints sitting outside the pub. By the time we'd landed they had gone in. My head bounced up into the roof so hard that my car had a lump like a little gun turret ever afterwards. It nearly broke my neck, too. And all because I was showing off to this lovely dark-haired girl.

And I didn't even learn my lesson then. Still showing off, I decided to go for a swim in the canal. I got my swimming trunks on and dived off the bridge. To my horror and surprise I found the water was only about two feet deep. I shot into mud at the bottom and a bloody great water rat swam across my face, and I couldn't get out fast enough. She was a very attractive girl but my mother had her eye on me all the time.

Around that time my mother and father decided to take life a little more easily. They had worked very, very hard running all the shops, usually a pub as well, and my father running his joinery business. They moved to Blackpool intending to ease into a sort of semi-retirement. Naturally my mother could not stop work just like that and she bought a small butcher's shop. I loved Blackpool. I loved the bustle, and the excitement of being near real showbusiness stars. I always wanted to entertain and as I got older it became my real ambition.

I was a great admirer of Frank Randle. I thought he was a brilliant comedian. I had great respect for George Formby, too. They used to have these wonderful seaside shows at the Opera House, which was where years later I was to do my own Royal Variety Performance. But then I could only dream from the audience. I was starstruck, and became more and more fascinated by the business of humour. I could watch these fine comedians for hours and thoroughly enjoy myself but never laugh. I was learning, and even then I knew that comedy is a serious business.

Sadly the real world intruded into my dreams. I told my mother that her little shop was not going to provide enough work for me. She suggested bluntly that perhaps I should go and get myself a job. I found one as butcher's assistant at Blackpool Co-op. In the afternoon all the young lads had the happy job of killing poultry and dressing it. We teamed up in pairs, one killing and plucking and the other one penning the poor creatures in. They gave us twenty birds each to do and the last four teams had to clean the place up. I only got caught for that the once, the first time, when I didn't realise what was going on. I teamed up with another fellow called Wormhole, you can't forget a name like that. I didn't enjoy the job much, I was beginning to think that I had seen just about enough butchering to last me a lifetime.

When I was twenty-one I inherited some
money from my great-uncle Hague. It was
£100 in war bonds and I thought I was a millionaire. I went out and bought a car, a fabu-
lous Armstrong Siddeley Sports, with an
automatic. It was smashing, even if it was
almost impossible to start on a cold morning.
It was advertised in a Blackpool paper for £50.
A lady was selling it; the car had belonged to
her husband who had died three months
before and she couldn't bear even to look at
it again.

Coming of age encouraged me to think of a
career change. Still enthused by my inheri-
tance I went to the Labour Exchange – the
only time I've ever been inside such an estab-
lishment in my life. I bought a nice new suit
and drove up in my nice car, looking smart. I
marched in and chirpily said, 'Do you think
you could find a job for me?'

They looked at me as though I was barmy,
and I explained that I'd been working for my
parents but that my mother had now retired. I
told them I was a competent butcher but

didn't want to do the job any more. Could they find me something else?

'Do you think you can sell stuff?' they asked. I liked the sound of that, and they suggested a job as a salesman for Carters of Sheffield, manufacturers of all things medical from bandages to cough medicine. That very afternoon I was introduced to the traveller for the Fylde area who told me somewhat haughtily that if he was to take me on permanently I had to find new customers. Yet when I asked him how long he had been selling in the area he said twenty years. I said, 'Surely after twenty years you've found everywhere there is to find?' He said, 'Oh no, there are still shops to find. But if you see any of our stuff in any of the shops, you must come straight out. They are my customers. I think you should be able to find about six customers a day.' I thought this was an amazingly tall order but I was determined to have a go at something different so I said I would give it a try.

I didn't have much idea what I was really selling, but I used my loaf. I went in to a chemist's and threw myself on the shopowner's mercy. I said, 'I'm sorry to bother you, I'm very new at this job. I come from Carters of Sheffield and this is my sample box. I haven't even opened it yet, I don't know what is inside. Would you mind having a look with me?' He laughed; my story seemed to intrigue him, and before I knew it the chemist was explaining what everything was. By the time we'd finished he had spent £2 with me and I was away. First customer, first sale. I thought, this is not bad. I worked that dodge in shops all around Blackpool. I got seven new customers that day, but I thought I'd keep quiet about some of them in case I didn't do so well the next day.

When I met the traveller in the evening I just told him I had four. 'Well, that's not bad,' he said quietly, but I could tell he was surprised I'd sold anything. Inside three months I had more customers than him. I found if I could make the shopkeepers laugh I was halfway to clinching a sale. I had found a job I liked and I wasn't cutting up dead animals any more. I was laughing, as usual.

A few months went by and the top people at Carters sent for me to go and see them in Sheffield. They explained to me that if I stayed with the firm for twenty-five years I would be on a good pension. I had no intention of spending twenty-five years going round shops, even if I did have the aptitude for it. But for once I kept my mouth shut.

I had really impressed the bosses by winning a cough medicine competition that ran for four weeks. I won all four times and got a £10 prize – not bad, flogging cough medicine in the sunshine. I encouraged all my customers to take it with a lot of discounting. So the bosses in Sheffield wanted to see this sales phenomenon, and they asked me to take over the whole of Kent. They told me the bloke working down there had been with them for twenty-three years and was getting past it. I said, 'So you're pensioning him off.' 'No,' smirked the bloke talking to me. 'I'm afraid he doesn't qualify for a pension as he is two years short.'

At that I stood up and said, 'Right. Thank

you for the lunch, gentlemen. I shall not be working for you any more.' I walked straight out of the place and they never saw me again. It just made me see red that they thought I would be impressed that they were kicking this poor sod out on his ear without a pension to make way for me. My mother supported me when I told her. She said, 'You must always stand up for what you think is right. You've done the right thing, principles are important in life.'

I reckoned that if I could sell pills and powders I could sell any bloody thing and I went selling motor cars. By then my mother and father had got fed up with semi-retirement in Blackpool and they had come back to Castleton, near Rochdale, and taken the George and Dragon.

So I went to Rochdale Motors and started selling cars. I sold seven cars on one Sunday alone. They had five salesmen, and they hadn't sold one car between them that week. I went back to Blackpool at the weekend to see a pal of mine who was a baker, and I went in an

MG sports car. He wanted to buy it. I told him it was for sale for £80. He bought it, and best of all he had a Vauxhall 14 to sell and we found a farmer that wanted that. It went like that all day. I had seven order forms on Monday morning.

I think my mother had done me a favour with her strictness because I was keen on work and I wasn't looking for girls; I was very interested in what I was doing. I would stand in the showroom until 10 or 11 o'clock on Saturday night to get a sale from people coming out of the pubs. I've sold cars to drunks. I often took good customers home to the George and Dragon for a drink to celebrate a sale. I would get them what they wanted and then shout, 'Dad, I'll have a whisky, please,' and he always knew to give me cold tea. Then the customer would get a round and I'd get another tea. And make sure I got the money for the whisky back later on. I got up to a lot of tricks in those days.

George Formby was getting very popular in the thirties and I remember buying myself a really beautiful ukulele which I have still got. I taught myself to play by using the sheet music they always had in the *News of the World* every week. I played a song called 'At the Masquerade'. One night at the George and Dragon the turn did not arrive. My father said, 'Do you think you could do something for us?' 'I'll have a go,' I replied and then it suddenly struck me what I'd said. I went to get my ukulele and broke my rule of not drinking by having a small whisky. I put my foot on this chair and I was that nervous my foot was doing a tap dance on the chair.

I started playing the song and I couldn't finish it. I just kept going over and over the same bits. That was my first experience of getting up and actually trying to entertain the public. When I came off I was in a muck sweat, and I thought that was wrong. Then I realised that what I had to do was mix a few of my stories in with the ukulele, because I could tell a story well even if I wasn't very good on the ukulele.

The experience made me determined to do better. Mind you, it wasn't exactly the most discerning audience. Most of them had had more drink than was good for them. I lived with mother and father in a lot of pubs and I think that put me off drink. When you've fetched drink up the cellar and helped to clean out the pumps on a Sunday morning, and you've seen blokes come out of the steelworks every night to the pub and spend all their money over the bar, it does make you a little aware of the dangers of drink.

One regular customer had about seven kids, and one of them would come to the door and pop his head round to say, 'Is me dad in? My mum says can we have half a crown so we can have some tea?' This bloke would snarl, 'He's not here again. All they want is money. Here's two shillings, tell her to make do with it.'

I used to think, what a shame. A nice family and all he did was work and then go and drink Old Tom, which is a very strong beer, and stagger home all over the place. I thought he must be mental. It put me off, seeing blokes fighting over nowt because they were drunk. My mother used to keep a shillelagh behind the bar and she would wade into action with it if there was any trouble.

I was always much too careful with my
money to want to waste it on drink. As a young
man I used to save half a crown a week in a
Wakes Club. Wakes were the Lancashire holiday time. At the end, with interest, I had
£6.17.6, and I had a week's holiday in Blackpool with that, and brought my immediate
family a present home each. I paid for my digs
and had a lot of fun. It sounds impossible but
I did it, a lot of people did. Bed and breakfast
was half a crown. Those were the days, they
really were.

My mother and father's fortunes went up
and down, but they always struggled. For all
the work and enterprise they put in they
should have done a lot better than they did,
but I think the problem was that they had two
distinct businesses. If they had concentrated
on just one I think they'd have done better. My
mother was a terrific businesswoman. My
father was nice feller, he could make people
laugh like me.

But there wasn't a fortune to be made in

pubs – when you think a gill of mild beer was twopence halfpenny, a pint of best mild was fivepence, bitter was sixpence. You could get canned on three shillings, so they didn't make a lot of money – there wasn't a lot of money to make. And you had to give people entertainment, and pay the wages. Blimey, I sound like Alec Gilroy.

After the Clarence they had a pub called the White Stone in Chadderton Road, then the Church Inn in Shaw, and the Blue Bell in Shaw and then, just before the Second World War, the George and Dragon in Castleton. But these were the years of the Depression and nobody was making a fortune; you were doing all right if you were making a decent living.

Coming from that sort of background helped me always to look on the bright side of life. And I've always been a lucky so and so. One tragic incident helped to bring that home to me most forcibly. When I was working at the garage I started having flying lessons, along with one of the other salesmen, a friend of mine called David.

One beautiful June day we were due to go up from Barton airfield for an hour's flight, and right at the last minute a customer came into the garage and I sold him a car. That made me late, and when I got to the airfield an aeroplane was just taking off. The mechanics who knew me said that David had gone up with someone else.

I turned round and drove back to Rochdale. On the way I saw a fire engine, and a fireman told me that a plane had come down in the hills between Oldham and Rochdale. I just knew it would be David. I felt sick.

I rushed to the scene of the crash and identified the bodies to the police. It was David and another poor lad whose name I never knew. I learned afterwards that the wing had peeled off and the plane had come down, decapitated the two of them, and impaled itself on a fence. My father had gone to Rochdale Theatre that night and when he came out it was all over the town that two car salesmen had been killed in a plane crash. He knew I was flying that night. When he got back home and saw me I thought he was going to drop dead. He was so shocked to see me alive. Next day it was all over the papers that I was the luckiest man alive.

I was devastated by the death of my friend, but all my life I have felt that someone was watching out for me. He certainly was that day.

CHAPTER Three

Wartime

WHEN I WENT OFF TO WAR my mother came to the station with me to see me off to Aldershot. Her parting words as the train steamed out of the station were, 'Goodbye son. Be a good lad and don't fight.'

I had to smile. Not that I wanted to fight anyone, I just thought it might be a bit difficult to avoid a scrap in wartime. I volunteered for the Army. I thought, if everybody stands back waiting to be called up, that's no good. I was very upset about the Germans trampling all over the place. I thought I'd have a go, and I don't think it was the wrong decision. A lot of people stayed out of the Army on some pretext or other and made a lot of money. I'm glad I went. I can wear my medals with pride.

I suppose, to be honest, I was being a bit selfish. I thought if I went in early I would be more likely to be able to choose what I did. I didn't want to be in the infantry, I preferred a mobile unit because I knew I could always drive. I opted for the RASC; being a volunteer I got that sort of preference.

When I went for my medical in Manchester the doctor looked at my records and said, 'You've had rheumatic fever. We can't use you.' I was absolutely crestfallen. I felt as fit as a fiddle. As if to make me feel better he added, 'I tell you what, young man, you've got the nicest feet I've seen.' Charming, I thought. If my feet are that nice why won't you let me march into action with them.

I was very disappointed. But I wasn't going to be kept out of the War that easily. I told my parents there had been so many would-be recruits there that I came away. Next day I went to Ashton barracks and blow me if the doctor there didn't pick me out for rheumatic fever as well. I was getting worried about this. The next day I went over to Bury barracks and it was the same doctor I had seen the first time. This time he looked at me and said, 'My, you're determined.' And he gave me a wink and said, 'OK, you're A1.'

It was an enormous relief, because I felt so

*My mother and father outside the
George and Dragon pub in
Castleton.*

*Young muscle man! Having
recovered from rheumatic fever I
took up physical training – and
this was the result.*

*William Waddington
senior, poised for pint-
pulling behind the bar of
the George and Dragon.*

*Lance Corporal
Waddington. A stripe
arrived after just a month in
the army.*

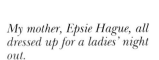

*My mother, Epsie Hague, all
dressed up for a ladies' night
out.*

A memory from the News of the World *in 1940 – I look more like a boy scout than a lance bombardier, but at least the cartoonist got the ukulele right?* (Cartoon: courtesy of the *News of the World*)

If you want to be a funny man, look funny. This was my first attempt at entertaining the troops.

Lovely Lilian, the Principal Boy who was just the girl for me.

Happy variety days – but I feel even happier wearing a cap!

I march into Europe – and get top billing! (Photo: courtesy of Stewart Darby)

*My favourite family photo, on the front at good old Blackpool, with
Lilian, little Barbara and Ann Denise.*

'Would you like to ride Lucy Lastic?' I asked the Princess Royal, with what the papers call 'Street cheek!'
(Photo: courtesy of Granada Television)

In the field with Diane Clay – my favourite female jockey – and my favourite racehorse.

'Bill Waddington, This Is Your Life!' I'm holding that famous red book, and if you look over my shoulder you can see Jill Summers, who plays Phyllis Pearce, standing what would be much too close for Percy's comfort!
(Photo: courtesy of Thames Television)

Congratulations to Lucy Lastic. She got her name because races always start with 'They're off!'
(Photo: courtesy of Provincial Press Agency)

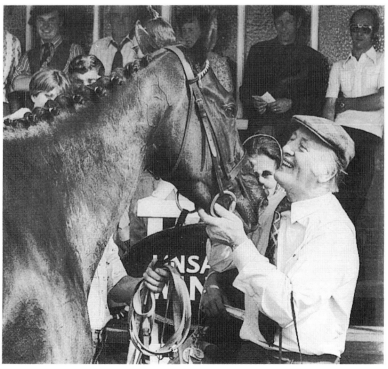

'Does that woman ever catch you?' asked Royal Street fan Princess Diana, at a Help the Aged event.
(Photo: courtesy of Help the Aged)

Although Percy and I both wear a cap, the similarity ends there. Relaxed and smiling at home in Cheshire, I share a joke with a good friend.

well. I was a very strong young man, physically strong, I could do a one-handed snatch and push on a bar bell of 120 pounds. I was very tough. Fellows a lot older would tackle me and finish up on their backs. I was never aggressive but I could hold my own with anyone. I had been taught boxing to help me get over rheumatic fever.

But after twenty-four hours in the Army in Aldershot I wished I hadn't tried so hard to join up. We were given the most revolting food I had ever seen – a disgusting meat pie served for some stomach-churning reason with fish gravy on. I thought, blow this, I don't mind fighting but I want feeding as well, so I went sick. I decided to get straight out so I fell back on my medical complaint. I felt a bit guilty about it but I thought, well, it's on your record, so use your rheumatic fever. I went to the MO and told him and he just shook his head. 'No, son,' he said. 'It says here you're A1. That's good enough for me.'

So I was stuck. And it was a real shambles at the start. Loads of us had no proper uniforms.

Some had grey flannels, a battledress blouse and a bowler hat on. They fitted us up the best way they could, but we looked a real Fred Karno's Army.

Right at the start I made a mistake because I had been told by an old soldier how to polish my boots. He used to come in my parents' pub and he'd been in the First World War. He showed me how to bone my boots – to rub little circles on the toecap with polish and then spit and polish and get your toothbrush out and rub it in very hard. That really made my boots shine. I did this for our first parade, for the want of something to do. It was the worst thing I could have done because the sergeant major walked right down through all the rows and then singled me out.

'Do you see these boots,' he barked. 'I want to see them all like this tomorrow. Everybody get your boots done like this. If you don't know how to do it, ask him.' Instantly I was the most unpopular feller in the bloody barracks. I was cleaning boots for hundreds of them. Then the very next morning we had an order of the day on the notice board: 'All boots will not be polished. In future they will be dubbined.' They had decided that the polish cracked the leather. So it was all done for nothing.

In under a week I was posted to a little village called Gillingham in Dorset and billeted in an old bone factory where they used to make glue. That was a little bit rough. We were sleeping on the floor, one blanket underneath and one on top. That was all we had and it was a freezing cold winter. In a very short time, with being in the cookhouse, I was promoted. I got a stripe, and I was a lance corporal, and then a corporal, and I was put in charge of the billet. There must have been a hundred men all sleeping on the floor and it was full of rats and mice and all sorts of creatures. I had very little hair then; at twenty-three I was almost as bald as I am now. But fellows next to me with good heads of hair found there were mice making nests in their hair at night. There was even a litter of little pink baby mice in one bloke's hair. For the first time in my life, I was glad I had gone bald.

We were supposed to be soldiers, but we were really just dressed-up civilians with no actual Army experience. We hadn't done any proper drilling and suddenly this prize specimen of a second lieutenant arrived. He had just been given one pip and seemed to be under the impression he was God. We had some very nice officers in the Army but he was not one of them. He just poked around everywhere in our billet trying to find fault, and he couldn't.

All of a sudden he looked at the windows. He said, 'Corporal, I shall be back in half an hour. I want to see all these windows properly cleaned.' I said, 'Are you sure, sir?' He said, 'Yes. Don't question my orders. Half an hour and I shall be back.'

We didn't do anything, we just sat around for half an hour until he came back. He said, 'Yes, that's better.' I said, 'Will you do me a favour, sir?' He said, 'What's that?' I said, 'Will you tap your stick on the window?' He couldn't, because there wasn't a window in the place. All the glass had been blasted out months ago. We used to wake up with snow on our blankets. He coloured up and marched out feeling, I hope, every bit as big a berk as we thought he looked. I had tried to put it in a nice way, and I think that cured him a little bit.

The one thing I missed in the Army was my dog. I had always had a dog. I had joined up from Castleton, and I'd already got a stripe when I went home to the pub on my first leave, so I felt very proud. The remarkable thing was that the day before I came home my little wire-haired fox terrier, Tab, sat behind the pub door all night, and my mother and father couldn't shift him. When I turned up the next day he went crackers. My father said, 'That dog knew you were coming.'

While I was at Gillingham I really started entertaining. I had taken my ukulele banjo with me and I spent every spare moment I had learning to play it. I was on parade one day and this sergeant major, who had seen me practis-ing, said, 'Waddington. That banjo thing. Can you play it?' I said, 'Oh, yes.' He said, 'Right, you're in the concert on Sunday.'

I was paralysed with fear. I knew I could play a bit and tell a story, but I didn't relish taking on an audience full of tough lads who were hardly in the mood for laughter. I thought, they'll tear me apart. But it all worked out well.

The concert was held in the local cinema, but it felt like the London Palladium to me. They didn't have a film on Sundays so we put a stage show on. I thought, I'll make myself look funny then at least I might get one laugh. I padded my stomach so I had a fat belly, then pulled my hair up to make it look even worse than it does, and slapped on a big false moustache. I thought if I wasn't that good at least I'd be hard for them to identify afterwards.

My mate Dougie Jordan came from Lancashire like me (he was the one whose auntie was a lady butcher like my mother – they were good friends). He was helping me to get ready for this show, and he was a bit worried about how frightened I looked. His remedy was a drink I had never encountered, the strangely named local delicacy 'scrumpy'. Dougie explained that it was only rough cider and assured me it would provide just the relaxation I needed. I was teetotal at the time but I was in serious need of assistance so I drank a glass. It was pleasant enough to drink. I said I didn't feel any different.

Dougie offered to fetch me another, so I had a second pint of scrumpy. Apparently shortly after this I made my stage debut. I don't remember the details but it seems I was a minor sensation. The major sent for me the following morning. He said, 'Waddington. Congratulations on your wonderful performance last night. It's rather a pity we had the ladies with us of course, but never mind.'

I hadn't got a clue what he was on about because I couldn't remember a thing about it. He went on to say that he was looking round for people of 'reasonable intelligence' – he didn't over-emphasise the intelligence – to earmark as officers to go to OCTU. But he continued, 'After seeing what you did last night I think you would be a lot more use to the Army as an entertainer to keep the morale of the troops up. That is going to be vital.'

I thanked him very much because I didn't want to be an officer, it was hard enough being a corporal.

I started organising events in the village for the lads because there was no entertainment for them. I put on dances, concerts and boxing shows. Dougie was put in charge of boxing. He could handle himself. That was more than you could say for his other friend, a corporal who came from Plymouth. He had worked in Plymouth abattoir humping meat. He was a big fellow, square and built like an outside toilet, as wide as he was high. We had had a few kerfuffles, him and I, because he was a boorish, ignorant man.

Dougie asked me if I fancied boxing against him. Dougie knew the chap would never touch me even though he was way out of my weight. I knew a bit about boxing, so I said, 'OK, put me down.' We squared up to each other in this village boxing tournament, a three-rounder. He was about three stone heavier than me but fortunately I was a lot faster than he was. If he'd ever hit me I'd have gone straight into orbit. I kept moving and clipping him, and by the end I had beaten this poor fellow quite badly. I was very sorry about it afterwards because he couldn't move, he was just like a punch bag. And when I saw him the day afterwards his face was a real mess.

Strangely, after that we became great friends. He came up to me and put his arms round me, and said, 'Well, you did what you had to do, and it hurt a bit, but not too much – but I'm not tackling you again.' We had half a pint of rough cider together and that was the end of it. By the way, I've still got the medal I won.

I much prefer joking to fighting, however, and there was a time when my ability to tell a funny story saved my life. I was on parade ready for embarkation shortly before the fall of Dunkirk. I was ready and waiting to be drafted overseas, but when the major saw me in the line-up as he was walking along doing his inspection he turned to his sergeant major and said, 'What's Waddington doing with these men?' The sergeant major explained

Chapter Three

that I had been drafted to France. The major snorted, 'He's not going, you know. What are we going to do at Christmas time in this dead-and-alive hole without him to amuse us? Send somebody else in his place.' So my entertaining abilities saved me from at least one perilous trip up towards the front line. I was extremely lucky.

In the early days of the war we were always very short of ammunition. When we went on manoeuvres we did not use bullets. Instead we were given instructions that if someone came up and pointed two fingers at us and said, 'Bang bang, you're dead', you had to be killed. As the war games went on, a young officer sneaked up behind me and said, 'Bang bang, you're dead.' I carried on walking. Again he said, 'Bang bang, you're dead.' I still didn't take any notice of him, so he came right up to me and said, 'Now look here, Waddington, I've said bang bang, you're dead twice. You should be dead.'

'Oh no, I shouldn't,' I told him. 'Can't you hear me ticking? I'm a tank!'

I put on the Christmas show, of course. I used to write all the shows and produce them. I did not know it at the time but it was tremendous training. At Christmas time, as a lot of the lads had now found girlfriends in the village, I got permission from the colonel for them to bring them in.

I was one of the lads who had found a girlfriend. I had met this attractive girl in Gillingham, a little bit older than me. Her father was the village police sergeant. I was in the village quite a bit, now that I was putting on all the entertainments for the troops down there, and I got chatting to her. She was called Evelyn Case and she was the first girl I was ever in love with. This was wartime remember, and I started thinking, I could go over to the other side and be dead and I will never have lived. I wouldn't have seen life.

I had had just about no experience of the opposite sex before I joined up, because of my mother's protective attitude. Even when I was eighteen she would insist if I was going to the pictures that I did not take a girl. She would say, 'Look, you've got to be up early in the morning to go to the market, you haven't time for that sort of thing.' I did know one or two nice girls that I was interested in, but I had to keep it a secret. So the first time I got away as a soldier I thought, 'right, now I can please myself.'

My mother thought I had too much to do to get involved with girls, and she wanted me to make a success of my life. When I told her that I wanted to make Evelyn my wife, she said, 'Don't you dare bring any girls here. Don't you dare.'

But my father wrote me a letter saying, 'Don't tell your mother I have said this, but if you like the girl, carry on. I'm afraid you'll never get anywhere with your mother.' My mother went on refusing to let me take her home. In a way I married Evelyn out of defiance of my mother, to be honest. I thought, well, you can't do anything about it. I'm of age, I'll marry the girl. But she still wouldn't let me take her home. I would have found out a lot more about her if I had. I'm like that, I can be a bit stubborn; if somebody says, you're not going to do that I say I will, just to show you I can, if it kills me.

I don't want to blame my mum but she was responsible in a way, because she wouldn't let me have experience of girls before I went in the Army. So when someone wanted to be with me and to talk to me I was very flattered. Evelyn was quite an attractive woman, that little bit older than me, and she seemed a nice person. She paid me some attention, and it seemed such a natural thing. I never touched her before we got married, never at all, because I was not that way. I wasn't looking for women other than for good friendship, somebody to dance with and somebody to be with a bit different from the young lads I was soldiering with. I was twenty-four when I got married. If I'd had any experience before then, I don't think I would have fallen in love quite as easily as I did. Anyway, as I say, I did it out of defiance.

So I married her. If I had had the guts on the day of the wedding I would have turned round and walked out of the church, because I got a message sent through from the hotel where my sister and her husband were staying in Gillingham. The landlord had been talking to them, saying that I shouldn't go ahead with this marriage. According to him, Evelyn had had a lot of boyfriends; he said that she was 'the pride of the village' and had been carrying on with the postman.

Almost straight away I knew it was a mistake. And as a marriage it was over just as soon as it started. But then I was moved away, to Hertford. Things weren't right between Evelyn and me so I was pleased to get away. We found a smashing billet there, and as soon as we arrived I found that they were putting on a Sunday night show at a big cinema. I had a bit of a reputation and they asked me if I would appear in the show. By then I had gained in confidence, I knew what I was doing and I didn't need to get drunk to get laughs.

The show went well, and the very next day that helping hand of good fortune that has followed me all my life waved into action.

The Blue Pencils concert party had arrived

to perform at a local hall in aid of the Army Benevolent Fund. The Blue Pencils were the first touring concert party of the Second World War, and they had soldiers and civilian girls in the show. Captain Benyon, who was in charge of the concert party, just happened to go across to the barber's to get his hair cut on the Monday morning after our little show on the Sunday night. He was busy telling the hairdresser about the Blue Pencils when the barber, bless him, said, 'You should have seen the fellow they had on at the cinema last night. He was hilarious. And clean too. You want to get him in if you can.'

That sparked the captain's curiosity. He asked around and found me, and asked my major if I would give an audition. I agreed and then found myself in front of Captain Benyon and his right-hand man, Sergeant Phil Merrick, a singer of some note who had appeared in the Royal Command Performance with Evelyn Laye before the war.

There were just the two of them sitting in this empty hall. I was on the stage by myself

107

and Sergeant Merrick just said, 'Right. Make us laugh.' And I did, even at 10 o'clock in the morning. Fortunately, even though I say it myself, I have a quick wit. I thought this was terrible, talking to a lot of chairs, and I took this pair into my confidence and pretended that at any minute someone else would be coming in and that I wanted to tell them all about me before anyone else arrived.

As an illustration I recalled an early encounter with a particularly aggressive sergeant major. He had said, 'Waddington, if you saw ten Germans coming towards you, what would you do?' 'Well, sir,' I said, 'if I had feet as big as yours I'd drop down into my boots and fire at them through my laceholes.' And I managed to get this pair laughing with nonsense like that.

Captain Benyon asked the War Office if he could have me in his concert party and that was such an important turning point for me. He got permission and I went into the show as principal comic and my life changed overnight. It was the best possible training ground for a life of laughter. I was touring the country with a busload of cheerful and talented entertainers. I simply couldn't believe my luck.

I was writing all my own material and struggling to come up with a new routine every night. Captain Benyon pointed out that if the audiences kept changing, the jokes could stay the same. It was a fantastic experience. Don't forget there was no television in those days, and often no theatre and no cinema either. So we were really made welcome when we arrived to put a show on.

I used to drive the coach as we hurtled up and down England, and our resourceful fixer, Inky Ingram, would go ahead and find us some marvellous places to stay. We were put up by the local gentry in some terrific houses. My standard of living was really on the up and up. Our patron in the Army was Brigadier General Nicholson, of Nicholson's gin fame. He was a real gent and used to come to the show every two or three weeks or so.

We had a wonderful electrician called Ronnie Keylock, who used to play the accordion in the show. Getting the power to run our floodlights was always a bit of a problem. In one Norfolk village he diverted so much electricity from the local houses to the village hall that he blacked out hundreds of homes. So the people had to come to the show. It was one way of packing them in.

I remember that incident very clearly because I was billeted in a lovely old cottage and the lady of the house was most attentive. She was about thirty-five. I've no idea where her husband was, or even if she had one. She cooked me some lovely grub and with all the rationing it was most welcome. However I did not expect her next move. Towards the end of the week, after supper she asked if I had enjoyed the meal and then she said, 'If you would like something else you know where my bedroom is.'

I was speechless! I didn't go up to my bedroom right away, but sat wondering if I had really heard her correctly. Then I went up and lay on my bed wondering if I should chance it. I thought, 'well, it's wartime. I could be dead next week and I've never lived.' Anyway I talked myself into making the effort.

All the curtains were pulled back in the darkness even though we had blackout regulations to conform to. There I was, in my pjyamas, with the moonlight glinting off my bald head, creeping carefully into my lady's chamber. She was fast asleep and I leant forward to tap her affectionately on the shoulder. Her eyes opened, and she saw me in the moonlight, and she let out a scream that must have woken half the village. I realised then that I had misunderstood. 'Something else' was never mentioned again.

On one much happier night our party put on a show in Baldock in Hertfordshire. The BBC arrived to put our concert out on radio and my very first broadcast turned out to be quite a hit. The national papers all noticed it. The *Daily Mail* reported 'Army Comedian is on the Road to Fame'. It was wonderful; I got my first reviews and they were all good.

I had written home to tell my mother and father I was going to be on the radio and they were all listening in the George and Dragon. Well, all except my father. He couldn't bear to listen. He was so nervous for me, he said, 'Oh no, I can't stand it. He'll make a mistake.' And he went up to the bedroom out of earshot. About halfway through the programme my mother shouted upstairs, 'Come down, Will, he's marvellous.'

That was the first of hundreds of radio broadcasts, and it was the most important. Before then I had been an ambitious amateur entertainer who could tell a few gags. After that I knew in my heart I was a comedian.

When I walked into the pub on my next leave home my mother and father were so proud of me. My mother said that on the night of that first broadcast my father had taken a bottle of Dimple Haig whisky, which was not easy to come by, off the bar shelf and said, 'I won't touch that until my lad comes home out the Army.'

They were marvellous times with the Blue Pencils. Everything changed for me when I joined the Army's first concert party. It was such a wonderful door opening for me to the entertainment business. I couldn't have had a better start, because I was working with people I could stand up with. They were talented, but they weren't fantastic pros because all the great big names were kept out of the war to entertain on a larger scale. So I had the chance to have a go without being overshadowed.

When Brigadier General Nicholson was given his bowler hat, as they describe retirement from the Army, he gave us a wonderful party. And he asked us if there were any secrets we had kept from him. Over this lavish duck supper I told him of the time I had briefly reached his rank. It was in Wolverhampton of all places, where we did a sketch in which I played a brigadier general.

We were so short of uniforms that my own best uniform was used as my costume, adorned with the red tabs, the crown and swords, and the rest of the insignia. As we were going on leave the next day I asked the officer in charge if I could get another uniform as my usual outfit was filthy due to shifting scenery. He was too busy to help and just brushed me off. The only thing I could do was to take my dirty uniform to the dry cleaner's in Wolverhampton. And the only uniform I had to wear in the meantime was the brigadier general's.

I took the risk and wandered around the town all morning receiving courteous salutes from a host of senior officers. My friend Sergeant Frank Myers was with me, and was petrified throughout. I must have looked the youngest brigadier general in the British Army by a mile.

Luckily, I took to broadcasting and I was quick enough to write my own material. I was often billed as the Army's number one comic and it was a title I was always determined to live up to. At one time they swopped me from concert party to concert party – I worked with the Mustard Pots, the Norfolk Turkeys. I was always being lent out because although the other concert parties had comics they weren't clean enough, and frankly they weren't very good. That got me in and I grabbed the opportunity with both hands. I did a lot of Ack-Ack,

Beer-Beer (for anti-aircraft, barrage balloon) shows on the radio. I always tried to find something new.

Clifford Davis, the journalist who went on to become showbusiness editor of the *Daily Mirror* and a regular panellist on New Faces, was a member of the Blue Pencils. He was quite a pal of mine. He came to write and to compere on our tours. I knew by then that my marriage was really over. I did go back to see Evelyn for Christmas leave but I got Clifford to send me a telegram ordering me to report back to my unit, so I was only there for twenty-four hours. It just felt all wrong. I didn't wish the woman any harm, I just wanted to be away from her. I knew I had make an awful mistake.

I got on quite well with Clifford until I found out that he had had a book of sketches published by Samuel French and he had included stuff of mine without permission.

I went mad, I was going to kill him, and he was a bigger fellow than me. I told him, if you ever do anything like that again I'll take my chances with you. I wouldn't have pinched any of his stuff – not that any of it was worth pinching. I had a right go at him. He was a pompous person and I think he was very jealous of me.

Captain Benyon took me to the back of the hall when Clifford Davis was compere and asked me what I thought. I said, 'He's stopping the show, and I don't mean with entertainment. He slows it up too much. The moment he came out on stage people hated him,' I said. 'He's spoiling the show.' And he was taken off. Naturally Clifford was not best pleased when he found out the nature of my advice. He was the worst compere I've ever seen.

There were so many marvellous moments with the Blue Pencils. I will always remember playing in my first big theatre, the Arts Theatre, Cambridge. I got tremendous publicity and we were honoured by a visit from the famous theatrical cartoonist Arthur Ferrier, whose cartoons of the big West End shows were carried in the *News of the World*. He did one of us which was very flattering, except that next to the sketch he wrote, 'Bombardier Bill

Waddington on his best Formby.' This saddened me because although I admired George Formby tremendously I did not want to look as though I was copying him just because I came from Lancashire and played the ukulele. I stopped playing the uke for quite a time after that. I wanted to be me and nobody else.

After a while the Blue Pencils' success was widely copied and concert parties began springing up all over the place. The Army thought things were getting out of hand and decided to weed them out. Unfortunately they weeded out the only flower as well and the Blue Pencils were no more. The concert parties were all amalgamated into what was called the Central Pool of Artists which became the Stars in Battledress, run by Captain George Black, son of the famous impresario with the same name.

At this time I was drafted to Drayton Manor at Fazeley, near Tamworth, back into the Army for real, although I was put in charge of entertainments there. I was also doing my share of soldiering, driving on convoys and other duties. All the concert parties stopped. But I put on a show once a week called 'Canteen Night' – the lads couldn't go out every night, they were only allowed out one night a week, so we put on some entertainment for them to keep them together and stop them from going absent without leave. I used to involve fellers that were new to the Army, who were a little bit skittish and would be off given half a chance. I would try to involve them in the show and grab their interest; that way we didn't have half the people running off.

I did a lot of gags, some of them with a purpose. I've always said that you can get things done better in life by having a laugh about them, treating problems in a humorous way, than by complaining grumpily and being a pain in the neck.

We had some young soldiers who came to us as very raw recruits. They were put on guard duty immediately after arriving. As guard commander I was alerted late one night by one of them shouting, 'Halt! Who goes there?' There was no reply and he shouted, 'Halt! Who goes there?' again. Then shortly afterwards I heard gunshots. The young fellow told me, 'It's over there, corporal. Over in the woods. There's somebody there.'

We investigated and of course there was no one there. It was just the trees blowing in the wind. But the adjutant for the day was a rather finicky fellow and he came down demanding to know what was going on. His decision was to take all the ammunition from the guards so this mistake could not happen again.

I thought this was a singularly daft move, even for an officer. But I said nothing – until the next concert, that was. Then I put in a gag about a soldier on guard duty challenging an intruder. I said, 'Halt! Who goes there? Halt! Who goes there? If you don't stop I'll go to the guardroom for a bullet.'

The place was in uproar as all the soldiers who thought it was crazy having people on guard in wartime without any bullets in their rifles yelled with laughter. The colonel was astounded. He couldn't understand what everyone was laughing at. But he soon found out and that adjutant found himself posted two days later. A little bit of comedy can do a lot.

We used to have competitions. One favourite was a quiz, with teams made up of drivers, NCOs and officers. I put the questions together. Some were straightforward, others were trick questions. We had a sergeant major who had been working on the railways at New Street Station in Birmingham. A big, big man, he was basically a bully, and he caused so much trouble among the lads. For some reason they looked to me to put things right.

I took a personal interest in taking him down a peg or two after he had me on a charge just because I hadn't had anybody on a charge. I wouldn't let anyone go out of the camp at night unless they looked clean and tidy with their boots shining and smart. I was the corporal in charge of the camp police. I was taken up in front of the major and I said, 'Can I just ask, sir, if anyone has been brought in from the town because they are improperly dressed? Because they don't get past me, sir, unless they look smart and their boots are clean. Could you walk out of this room and have a look round the camp and see if there is any litter, because I think you'll find there isn't. If I see anybody drop anything I make them go round the camp and pick up all the other rubbish, so they don't drop litter.'

The major pooh-poohed my charge and said forget it. So this sergeant major had his knife into me after that because I had shown him up for what he was, a bloody idiot. A few nights later I was organising one of my quizzes and this sergeant major came up to me and said, 'I want to be in the officers' team tonight, Waddington.'

I said, 'You're not an officer, sir, you're an NCO.' 'They're one short,' he barked gruffly. 'I'll go in with them.' There was no stopping him, so I decided to set up a special question for him. Bearing in mind that we were a motorised unit, and our job was to work out journeys and travel, the question shouldn't have been too difficult.

What he was asked was: 'We will now pretend that Tamworth from Fazeley is two miles. A man drives off in a wagon from Fazeley to go to Tamworth. He travels three times faster in the first part of the journey than in the third part of the journey and it takes him one hour. What is his average speed?'

He looked baffled and said, 'Can you say that again?' I repeated it. He puzzled for a moment and then he snarled angrily, 'That's not a fair question.' I said, 'All right, I'll pass it over to the drivers.' They burst out laughing and said two miles per hour. The major was there, and he looked at this berk and thought, what a dimwit. Soon afterwards he was posted. That got rid of him.

At one concert we had a visiting singer to entertain us. She was a huge woman, she must have been about fifteen stone. She had a quite nice contralto voice, but when she started singing 'I'm a little bird' a fellow from the back shouted, 'I wouldn't like to clean your cage out.' It brought the house down. I felt so sorry for the poor woman, but it was the best laugh of the night by a long chalk.

I was still doing quite a lot of broadcasts from Fazeley. They used to let me go down and do the Ack-Ack, Beer-Beer shows; I think I did more appearances on those than anybody else. I would go once every fortnight or three weeks. I loved it, and the lads used to like me going as well because I used to get paid seven guineas, and we could *all* have a night out with that.

Then we practised on the firing range, and I found I wasn't a bad shot. I got three bulls and two inners out of five shots. The next thing, and it frightened the life out of me, was a list on the daily board for the following people to attend further target practice to become snipers. I was on the list, and I was horrified. I didn't want to be a sniper, picking people off from up in a tree. So when we went on the next shoot I said, 'I didn't hit all that, you know. It must be one of those mistakes.' To make sure I did not get to be a sniper I put a bullet into each of the targets at either side of me so they did well. Everyone was kept on except me. I never wanted to kill anything, let alone people.

When I joined Stars in Battledress I found myself in impressive company. Arthur Haynes, Charlie Chester and Janet Brown were some of the leading lights, and I was proud to be among them. Of course the main preoccupation for all of us was the invasion of Europe. As the Allies gradually turned the tide of the war it was obvious to all of us that the next big step was across the Channel.

As the build-up to the assault into Europe went on we were moved down to Folkestone. It was all very hush-hush. There were twenty-five of us Stars in Battledress living in tents just outside the town. We were going across with the Scots Guards. Arthur Haynes was among us. We all used to meet in this tent after lunch, and Arthur and I set up a game of cards. There wasn't a lot else to do. You couldn't go into the town, so we made our own fun. We used to play poker. Arthur was a smashing fellow and a bit of a joker. One day he dealt the cards and when I picked up my hand I couldn't believe it – I had four queens. We only had peanuts but we started to bet. Nobody would put their hand down, we all kept betting.

Then the bugle went for an assembly and we had to get up and go on parade. Arthur said, 'All right, put your hands down and best hand wins.' We did that and everybody had four of something and a brilliant hand. Arthur had set it all up for a laugh. We finished up scrabbling around trying to get our money back. We had only waited in Folkestone for a few days when the order came to head for the docks.

Dunkirk had been a disaster and yet it was wonderful the way we got people out. The Germans could never defeat that sort of spirit, the British people have great strength of character. We never know when we're beaten, we always carry on. And now we were going back. Some of the lads with us had been through Dunkirk and they were leading us all back into it, saying, 'Right, it's our turn now.'

We went across on these motor torpedo boats bouncing up and down like shuttlecocks in the Channel. They were diesel driven and the smell of the diesel and the movement in the water made a lot of the lads extremely sick. Arthur was very ill.

The sick lads were down in the bottom of the boat. I wouldn't go down, I stayed on deck. I had done a lot of horse riding and I think that helped. I just rode it like I would a horse. On deck they had a great heap of tins of soup, and in the middle of each tin there was a wick made of gun cotton. You lit this and as it burned down it heated your soup. I loved this. I had about four tins because most people were too ill to eat. It was a wonder some of them could walk, let alone fight, when they got over. We came ashore on what they call DUCKS which could come out of the sea to land and drive up on to the beach. We went as far as Sommerview on the way to Bayeux, where we found an old monastery that had been battered by bombs and went down into the cellar to find a billet.

Occupied France was a big shock to me. I was very sorry for the children in Normandy. While the Germans had been there they hadn't been properly fed. Kids would come up begging. 'Cigarette for Dadda, chocolate for Mamma, you jig-a-jig Mamma for chocolate.' And they knew what they were saying as well.

We had a mess tent just outside Bayeux, and the kids would be delving into the swill bins. I couldn't stand this and I went out and gave these kids nearly all the food I had off my plate. But that landed me in great trouble. The officer of the day spotted me and he went mad. He said, 'Don't you realise what you're doing? There'll be crowds of them round here tomorrow. I know you feel sorry for them, we all feel sorry for them. But if you do that there'll be trouble.'

He was right. The next day there were twice as many children and they all came looking for me. I said, 'No. Big trouble for me.' But it broke my heart.

We did some shows in Bayeux in this old cinema which was designed just like Shakespeare's Globe Theatre. It was a very easy theatre to play. For the first Army show they brought some troops in. There were some people in a box, but I didn't know who the heck they were.

At the end of the show I said, 'Well, thank you very much, boys, it's been smashing working with you. I hope you've enjoyed the show. If you have, when you get back to the camp tell everybody you've seen the Stars in Battledress show directed by Captain George Black. If you didn't like it, tell them it was ENSA.' And it was the boss of ENSA in the box.

On another ship they had brought some pianos over for us, believe it or not. They were little mini-pianos in great big wooden boxes made with timber about two inches thick. When we got ours out of the box we went and had a rehearsal in one of the bombed-out rooms. We had a black lad with us called Cyril Lagey, a very funny man. I hoped at the end of the war I could get him to come and partner me. We would have been a sensation. Unfortunately we lost touch, and to this day I don't know what happened to him.

Cyril was frightened in the monastery, not just of the Germans like we all were, but of ghosts or evil spirits. So he went outside and slept in this box the piano had arrived in; until the shrapnel started drumming on the outside. He forgot about the spooks then and shot back into the house.

We saw quite a lot of France; we also saw the bombing of Caen when they had the 2000 bomber raid – two waves of a thousand bombers. It was the biggest raid of the war, with fighter accompaniment. I was standing up on the top of this old bombed-out monastery and we were bouncing up and down with the amount of bombs they were dropping, one wave from left to right and then another from right to left, and there was very little reaction from the Germans.

They were very well entrenched because they had been there for so long. It was a real stumbling block for the Allies; the Germans were fortified in every direction – like the bloke in a pill box with a machine gun – you'd get ripped to bits if you tried to march past; so they flattened the whole place. But the Germans had gone. We still bombed it because if we hadn't they would have come back. The bombs flattened everything.

Within two or three days of that I was up on a makeshift stage trying to do a show for the Allied troops who had just moved in, and the only thing that I could see that hadn't been hit was the hospital. It had a few pock marks on the walls but it was substantially intact, which was astonishing if you saw what a pasting that place took.

I didn't sleep properly for about the first five weeks of the invasion. But as soon as we could we started entertaining. We would use the corner of a field, an old farm building, anywhere. It was all very much on the spur of the moment.

One day we came across these troops and offered their captain an hour's fun. He was very keen for us to cheer up his men but he said, 'Before you start, we have been having a little bit of trouble with a German fighter pilot who keeps coming over and strafing our camp every evening at six o'clock.'

We went off and had our food and pulled our lorry under some trees. Then I heard the noise of this plane coming. Our boys had lined up anti-aircraft guns at 500-yard intervals and they were waiting for him. Boom. That was the end of that German. 'Right,' said the captain cheerily, 'now let's have that concert.' So we set ourselves up in an apple orchard.

In those days I always wore a very funny costume. I had a knitted bathing suit which hung right down on me – the crutch finished at my knees – a tin hat, these great big boots and my ukulele. And the ukulele had multi-coloured ribbons hanging off it.

This outfit of many colours I was wearing, well you could see it for miles. And here we were, doing this show on the back of a lorry in a Normandy orchard, and this young officer got up on the back of the lorry and shouted to his men, 'Now chaps, keep right under the trees, please. Keep well out of sight. You know the Germans will strafe anything they can see. So keep still and enjoy the show.'

I listened to this speech from my position on the back of the lorry and I felt just like a dartboard. I looked round at my audience and said squeakily, 'I won't be here long. I do a very quick act. Before you've had a chance to hate me I've gone.' And that day I introduced what was literally a running gag. Every time I heard a plane I jumped off the stage and rushed under the lorry. It got laughs every time.

I found myself getting hardened to scenes of injury and death. Friends died, but it was part of war. One of the things which saddened me the most was the way the animals suffered, particularly the horses. They would blow up like big balloons with methane gas and occasionally they would explode. The stench was dreadful. Horses are remarkable creatures. Once they have experienced a bombing raid and come through unscathed they are not frightened of the next one. They ignore it and carry on grazing.

There were just so many sad scenes. I remember once at an aerodrome one of our lads was dancing around, doing a soft-shoe shuffle on the ground, and a German soldier's foot came up out of the soil. They were just shallow buried there. It was chilling.

We used to go round in a lorry with our concert party entertaining different lots of troops. One day we were going down this road and suddenly I felt very uneasy. It was just too quiet. I said, 'Stop. There's something wrong.'

We got out and had a look round, and we saw a sign saying 'Achtung! Minen' which had been overgrown by the hedgerows. That road was mined with Teller mines, so going back over wheelmarks we had just come up was no guarantee you'd get back safely. If there was a mine under the ground, you could hit it ten times and nothing would happen; the eleventh time, up it would go. I was petrified, but we managed to get back and nothing happened.

It was hard being an entertainer in wartime. The most difficult job I ever had in my life was entertaining a tank brigade that had just had a pasting from a German panzer division.

There were only about twenty of them and it was the first time they had seen death. They were in shock and I was sent up there with an accordionist to try to bring them out of it. It was terrible. I couldn't do it for long. I did

133

what I could but by the time I'd finished I was in shock with them. That was in Normandy just after the invasion. A bit frightening was that.

You had to have gags ready for any emergency. You would be working on a makeshift stage and suddenly shells would start landing or aircraft would approach. If we heard tanks going past I'd say, 'My God, the Russians are here'; because it could kill your act, apart from any other more substantial damage.

It was in Bayeux that I thought I had found the dream billet. It was a cottage with some bunk beds upstairs and straw palliasses downstairs. So I told my lads, this will do for us. Arthur Haynes came in as well. We were all desperate for a good night's rest. In the middle of the night Arthur came to me and said, 'I'm being bitten something rotten.'

I looked at him – he was covered in flea bites. He wouldn't go back to his bed, so we just had to wait until morning to find out what was biting him. As dawn broke we saw the cause of the problem – the whole downstairs floor was covered with French tramps. And it stank to high heaven. Arthur was so badly bitten they had to send him home.

Charlie Chester came out with another unit as a replacement for Arthur and we became great friends. Charlie was a great one for making up stories. He wrote a gag to go with my bald head: 'I've had everything done to try to cure my baldness, but this doctor wanted to put a ferret up my nose to chase the hairs out.' Thanks, Charlie.

There were many strange coincidences and surprises in wartime. I got one of my biggest shocks in Normandy when I met a cousin I hadn't seen since I was a little boy. He was an NCO, and he immediately invited me to join him in the sergeants' mess, which in this case was a three-ton lorry. We poured an enormous excess of whisky down our throats that night as I went through every joke I could recall, and invented quite a few more.

On the way back to our billet I dragged my cousin and a fellow sergeant who was helping me home into a ditch. I was very ill. But the lads were all very good, and they knew I might be sick, so they got this biscuit tin my mother had sent me and put it under my face. I slept with my head leaning so hard on this tin that you could still see the mark it made three days later. That was the first night I had slept properly since we landed. There were so many disturbances going on – tanks going through, planes overhead. It was a tough time to be an entertainer.

As the advance towards Berlin went slowly on we reached Brussels. And we spent quite some time there. We were still in the Belgian capital when the Germans tried to break through at Christmas time. We had drafted a couple of women into our concert party by then; we had a soubrette singer, a Jewish girl. Her stories brought home some of the horror of the people we were fighting, and it did concentrate our minds for a few weeks.

My mother might have been a hard taskmaster and a bit strict on my lovelife but she was a very caring woman. In one of her parcels to me she had sent a bar of Dr Lovelace's Soap, an excellent product which happily came wrapped in black and white greaseproof paper.

In Brussels we had a night off, but as usual we hadn't any money, until I had an idea. The old £5 notes were white in those days, and this greaseproof paper was printed in black and it looked a bit like a fiver. So I trimmed the wrapper down to the size of a note and cleaned all the soap off it. It seems very dishonest now but I thought, 'Here we are, saving their lives, and we can't go and have a night out.'

Five of us went in to this hotel and I shouted, 'This is an English five pounds, can I change it?' The bloke gave me 500 francs, so we had one hundred francs apiece. We had a night out and we bought wristwatches and all sorts, all thanks to this soap wrapper. I thought, we could all be dead tomorrow. Why not?

I think the pressure and the horror of what I was doing gradually started to take its toll on me as the end of the war approached. I found myself in hospital in Epsom, very down and physically bruised by it all. But humour is a very powerful medicine. In the hospital there was a young Polish airman who had been very badly shot up. He didn't speak a work of English so we couldn't really communicate with him. But I was doing my routines in the wards to try to bring some cheer to the place and so there was a lot of laughter. One night he was nearby and as the gales of laughter built up we realised he was laughing with us. He didn't know why, but he was coming out of shock, and it was laughter which helped him to do it.

A period of recuperation soon put me back on my feet, but I had decided I'd had enough soldiering. Germany was beaten and I thought I had done enough – six and a half years for very very little. I went in to see the discharge panel and told them I thought it was time I got out of it now.

There was a colonel on the panel who said, 'What have you been doing during the war?' I thought, bloody hell, after all I've been through. I just said, 'Oh, messing about here and there,' as casually as that. He said, 'Do you know who you're talking to?' I said, 'No, I don't, I'm just answering a question.' He just looked round and the others all nodded and I was out of the Army. In return for risking life and limb on the battlefields of Europe I was handed a gratuity of just £85. Not the greatest booking I've ever had, but perhaps one of the most eventful.

I went and got my demob suit. Everybody had chalk-stripe suits and I wanted to be different. I got a check suit and it was hideous. And I got a trilby. Oh God, it looked as if it was made for a pet dog, it was a terrible trilby. And when I went back to my unit for my discharge they were all laughing at me. I thought, that's good, keep laughing; that is my business now.

When I got home my father looked at me and I said, 'It's over for me, Dad.' He said, 'What a bloody awful suit.' I laughed and said, 'Yes, I'm going to give it to one of the lads in the taproom.' He shouted, 'That's me finished for the night, Mother,' and he took his Dimple Haig bottle of whisky off the shelf where he'd saved it and he sat on the stairs and drank it all, neat. He never asked anybody to have a drink, he just poured it down himself.

CHAPTER FOUR

Lilian

IT WAS HARDLY THE MOST ROMANTIC CIRCUMSTANCES in which to meet the love of your life, dressed as Wishee-Washee the pigtailed Chinaman in preparation for a pantomime in Swindon. But I didn't care. The first time I set eyes on lovely Lilian Day, the panto's pretty principal boy, I never thought I was in with a chance anyway.

Why would a beautiful creature like that take any interest in a bald-headed little ex-Army comic like yours truly? It was my first pantomime after the war and I had thrown myself into a whirlwind of work to get my career into action.

The day I met Lilian I was racing round trying to fit in two performances at sunny Croydon, a radio broadcast for the BBC at Marble Arch, and the first rehearsal for the panto. So I wasn't exactly relaxed.

I noticed straight away what an attractive woman she was but I did not imagine she would look twice at a joker like me. Anona

Wynn was directing the pantomime. I was so busy I scarcely knew what day it was.

I went down to the band call at Croydon, then I rushed back into town to do the band call for the evening radio broadcast. Then I went to the rehearsals for the pantomime and that is when I got my first sight of Lilian. I thought, what a nice person. She had a lovely smile and she seemed so gentle, almost serene somehow.

But I had to dash back off to the Croydon Empire and then come back in to Marble Arch for the radio. As I was finally walking into the studio – I had already rehearsed my verse and chorus – the floor manager said, 'Forget your verse, we're short of time, just do your chorus.' I started singing the chorus only to find that the orchestra was playing the verse. So I had to get all that put right. Like I said, it was an incredibly hectic day.

That night as I tried to unwind, I had Lilian's face in my mind. But I thought she was bound to have a husband, a smart girl like that. As the week went on I saw quite a lot more of her and that shy smile of hers gave me a feeling I'd never had before.

The week after that we moved down to Swindon to perform the pantomime down there. I was the principal comic. But I still didn't seem to have time to get to know Lilian better. After rehearsing all day I was rushing off to Reading where I was appearing in the theatre twice nightly as a comic on the bill with Henry Hall and his Band.

Henry Hall's principal singer was Betty Driver, now better known as Betty Turpin in Coronation Street, so I actually met Betty and Lilian in the same week. Betty was a very kind girl, and she had an equally kind friend with her, called Eva Benyon. I used to come up to Reading on the train as I couldn't afford a car then, and when I walked into the theatre they always had a cup of tea waiting for me. They knew I'd been rehearsing all day and had had a long journey and they looked after me as though they really knew me well.

So it is just possible that if Lilian hadn't been there at the time I might have married Betty. I

had blotted my first marriage completely out.
Evelyn had her life and another man and that
was all over for me. I was determined to make
it in the business and marriage was certainly
not on my mind.

But Betty was a strikingly attractive woman
and we got on very well. Flashing forward to
the present day, we still do in Coronation
Street. These days I always joke that she has to
lose two and a half stone before we can marry
and she always reckons she's halfway there.

I think that for all my endeavours that week
I earned £65, which was an awful lot of money
in those days. I got back to Swindon and got
paid on the Saturday night, and as I couldn't
get to the bank I wrapped my money in a handkerchief and left it in my pocket in my dressing room. When we rehearsed on Sunday I
went to get my cash and found just an empty
handkerchief. Someone had stolen all my
money. The only person that could have
known about it was the man that was dressing
with me, but I couldn't prove it. I had worked
all that bloody week for nothing. But in my

heart I knew I was in profit because I had met Lilian.

Wally Patch was Abanazer and Tom Paine was Widow Twanky. Tom was a bit jealous of my billing, because he had been on the variety stage for a long time whereas I'd come to it via radio and the war. He had never seen me working. I noticed that a little bit of an edge crept in, but it didn't worry me. I just carried on and did my stuff.

Lilian was staying in digs and I was in an hotel not very far away. I offered to walk her home, just friendly. I was never one of those blokes who are very forward with women. The panto went on for about six weeks and her mother came down to see a performance. We were going off down to Folkestone, and I carried their bags to the station which went down well with her mother.

She said, what a nice young man – they weren't used to being looked after like that. And our relationship built up very quietly from that. We got settled in Folkestone, and we happened to be staying in the same digs this time. We had our separate rooms, of course, but we had our meals together and we gradually got to know each other a bit better.

I remember one night we were having a meal and the landlord came in and said, 'I'm afraid my daughter is having a baby in the next room, so don't be alarmed if you hear some screaming or unusual noises.' We felt sorry for this poor girl. It seemed a shame that this was the only room they had available for her. Lilian never forgot it, and in a funny way it brought us closer together.

Then her mother invited me up to stay with them in Leicester, and of course I accepted. I was working at Chester in variety at the time and by then I had bought a car. But I had met another very pleasant woman on the train and we were friendly, though nothing serious. I invited her to come and see the show on the Saturday.

But on the Friday night I rang Lilian in London to find out if she was going to be home in Leicester for the weekend, and couldn't reach her. So I rang her mother, who didn't seem to know where Lilian was going for the weekend. I said, 'Have you any idea?' I was worried and jealous all at the same time. 'I think she is going to Brighton,' said her mother. That rang alarm bells for me. I thought, I wonder if she is going to come here and surprise me and I have got this other woman coming.

So now I started trying to put this other woman off. I told her I couldn't get her a ticket, that the place was booked. In the end Lilian didn't turn up and neither did this woman. But I never slept a wink on that Saturday night because all the pounding of my heart had made me realise how much I thought of Lilian.

Next morning I got in my car and drove to Leicester like a maniac. I got there and knocked on the front door and I couldn't believe how relieved I was to see her there. The family made me most welcome and our love sort of built up from there on.

I don't think I ever got down on one knee and proposed to Lilian, though nothing would have given me greater pleasure. I just said one day, 'When my divorce comes through I'll marry you, if you'll have me.' She said, 'Of course I'll have you.'

I bought a big touring caravan and she used to come with me all over the country. Lilian didn't want to be away from me. She wanted to be with me all the time. She was in the act for a time. She would come on halfway through and demand the suit back that I'd borrowed.

But I was still trapped in this unhappy marriage, which I very much wanted to get out of. I had no interest in seeing or hearing from my wife again. At first Evelyn wouldn't budge, so I gave her grounds. I let her know that I was going out with Lilian and that was the end of the road.

Even my mother approved of Lilian. She said, 'Ah. You've met your Waterloo now.' I said, 'Yes, but I should have met her at Euston. The train was late.' By then I could joke with my mother and get away with it. I told her Lilian was the woman I loved and that was that.

We got married in the registry office at

Newcastle-on-Tyne on a Saturday morning and
had our honeymoon in London where I was
top of the bill at the Collins Theatre, Islington.
It was a very old music hall, but I never turned
work down. A lot of people wouldn't go to
what they called number two theatres. I didn't
care; I would have gone to number seven if
they paid me the same money. That's what
kept me working, I'm sure. And that was the
only honeymoon we ever had because I never
stopped working.

Fortunately Lilian's parents were used to
the nonstop flurry of showbusiness life. Her
father, George Seymour, had been on the
stage himself. He had been to America in the
Mumming Birds with Charlie Chaplin and
Stan Laurel. But he didn't like the States so he
quickly came back. Lilian's mother was a
charming lady. We never had a cross word. She
had a job during the war in the Army pay
corps, which was in Leicester. Whenever I was
staying nearby I used to cruise up in the big
flash car I ran then and pick her up.

I still did a lot of mother-in-law gags after I

was married, and people who knew her used to come up and say, 'Oh, you are rude about your mother-in-law! She is such a nice lady.' I used to say, 'It's not her, it's my stage mother-in-law I'm talking about.' We did get on extremely well. She told me later that Lilian had had lots of admirers but usually after she had seen them two or three times she didn't want to know. Her mother used to get sick of going to the door to these young men and saying, 'I'm sorry, she has gone out,' when really she was at home reading the paper. She just didn't want to know. Her mother said Lilian talked more about me than anybody she had ever known.

Those years just after the war were very difficult for many people. Families were wrenched apart by all the turmoil, and jobs and money were hard to come by. But for me they were marvellous years. At last I had found the sort of woman I had only dared to dream about. And I seemed to have launched my career successfully.

In the hospital in Epsom I had befriended a young man called Norman Newell who

cleaned buses for the council in London. I was
writing little ditties for pantomimes hoping to
sell them. I had my ukulele with me. Norman,
who was just two beds away, said, 'I would love
to write songs.' I told him to go away and write
a song about Cinderella. 'I know them all, so
you can't kid me,' I told him. In twenty minutes he was back. There was no music in his
voice at all, but the lyrics were brilliant and the
basic melody was fine.

We soon got friendly. I really thought he had
something, and we started writing little bits of
tunes. I was into song-plugging in those days. I
used to get £25 for plugging a song on the
radio, which was much more than the fee for
the broadcast – it was a fortune to me. I knew
a man called Syd Coleman from Cinephonic
Music and I suggested to Syd that he put Norman in a shop selling sheet music so that if
someone came in with a good melody and a
bad lyric they could let him have a look at it.
They gave him a job in Charing Cross Road. I
knew he had talent.

Norman had been earning £2 10.0 a week

cleaning buses, and he went up to £10 straight away in the music shop. That was a lot of money. We kept in close touch for a while and whenever I was on in London I would get him to come to the show and introduce him to anyone I thought might help him. I'd say, 'Look, Dorothy Squires is on the bill, you might be able to plug her a number.' He went on to become head of Decca and head of HMV.

Just after leaving hospital I had some dates in London, then I had a booking in Aberdeen and Norman came to help me get my bags on the sleeper at Euston. I had been doing very well, but I knew I was moving into a different market now, talking to Scottish people. I got these digs in Aberdeen in a great big granite house. My landlady asked whether I liked kippers. I must have nodded because I had them roasted, boiled, standing up, lying down, fried, or boiled for every meal.

I was busy writing a script for a broadcast I was to do in a fortnight's time because you had to submit all your scripts to the BBC in advance. Maybe my mind wasn't totally on the job, or maybe it was just inexperience, but I went on stage at Aberdeen and I think I really died that night. It was the only time it happened to me. They just didn't know what I was on about and that was totally distressing for me because I had been doing so well everywhere. I went back to my digs and sat and thought how to get through to these people.

I was second top of the bill and I got so upset that I put cotton wool in my ears when I came off stage so that I couldn't hear if anybody else did well with applause. I couldn't stand it. I did a little bit better second house but all week I really struggled. It was awful. Until Friday night, when I went on and I paralysed them. I got such a laugh when I went on I thought my flies were undone; I have never done so well in my life. Second house I paralysed them again. I went back to my digs, and I thought I hope she had some kippers ready for me. But the first thing my landlady said was, 'Are ye no going down to the docks?'

I said, 'What do I want to go down to the docks for?' 'To see the fireworks,' she said. 'It's

VJ night, the war's over.' I didn't believe it. Of course that was why I had gone down a bomb, because everyone was so relieved the war had finished. Next night I went back on to silence.

Back in London I realised I needed a more professional approach if I was going to make a success of this business. And I needed an agent. Long before the war had ended I had decided that when peace finally broke out I was going to do my damnedest to start a career in showbusiness. Nothing gave me more pleasure than to make people laugh. The first time I made a room full of people laugh I felt a thrill of exhilaration that I have never tired of. I loved entertaining in the Army, so I wanted to do it for real.

When I first came out of the Army, an American called Charlie Tucker, who had been a big pre-war agent, sent for me. Charlie had been a big noise in London in the 1930s but he quickly skipped back to America when hostilities started because he thought the rough stuff might reach London. When the war was over he wrote me a letter saying that George Black, who had been my captain in Stars in Battle-dress, had strongly recommended him to get hold of me.

I went to see Charlie in his magnificent office. He was sitting behind a desk about the size of a football pitch and he said, 'You come very well recommended by the Blacks. I think you are going to go places. Next time you're in London let me know and I'll come and see your act.'

I said, 'So the recommendation is not good enough, then. The next time you see me working in London I will have been booked by someone. And if they have booked me on the recommendations I have had, I shall stick with them. I'm sorry, but that's it.'

My problem was that although I was well known on radio thanks to all my wartime work, I was a voice and not a face. I knew I needed to get showdates in London.

I went down to Southend-on-Sea and did the sort of routine that had always tickled the funny bone of the troops. As usual I was heavily made up. Cissy Williams, the all-powerful chief booker from Moss Empires, gave her important verdict; she said, 'He's not quite ready for us yet and he doesn't need all that make-up.'

In the meantime I had been to see another agent in Blackpool called Hymie Zyal. He asked me how much I wanted a week. I thought for a moment and then answered £55, which was a lot of money then. He laughed me out of the office and said, 'You've got to be joking.'

My next date was at the Bedford Theatre, Camden Town, as the comic on the bill with Ivy Benson and her Girls' Band. That afternoon I went down the Charing Cross Road and bought myself a smart suit and a smart hat from Cecil Gee's. The outfit cost me £36. For the first time in my life I went on the stage smart and just as myself, without any funny make-up, joke moustaches or silly props. And I paralysed them. It went down a bomb. I couldn't believe it, it went so well.

In the interval I was sent for, and I went to the bar and there was a little Scottish comic whom I can't name for the life of me. He had heard about me going to Hymie because Hymie had told everyone how much I'd asked for. The bar was full of agents and the little comic shouted out, 'Hymie, ask him how much he wants now.' Hymie was fuming and the little comic came up to me and said, 'Smashing, that's stuffed them good and proper. They didn't expect that.' I booked nearly five years' work that night in that bar.

But I still needed an agent and the large and respected firm of Richards and Marks approached me. They had an impressive office in Mayfair and seemed very nice people. I was flattered when they wanted to take me on their books. I stayed with them for quite some time. Sadly David Marks died, but the man who was virtually running the office by then, David Murray, and Johnny Riscoe, a very good ex-performer, linked up with Lew and Leslie Grade, and they took me with them.

They were marvellous. I worked with them for more than twenty years and I never signed a contract with anybody; I didn't have to. I just

used to say, if you don't trust me don't have
me. I trusted them, so there was no need for a
contract. We shook hands on a ten per cent
deal and that was our agreement. In those days
you would get your fee and your agent would
send you an invoice and you would pay him his
ten per cent. Nowadays that's all changed.
They generally take their cut straight away –
and often it is fifteen, or twenty, or even
twenty-five per cent. Agents have become very
greedy. The Grades weren't anything like as
big then as they became. They grew and I grew
with them. Lew and Leslie gave me a warm welcome and they found me some very very good
work. And when they started bringing all the
big American stars over, like Lena Horne, I was
the comic on the bill.

I arrived at the kamikaze booking for English comics, the Glasgow Empire, as the comic
on the bill under Dorothy Lamour. She was
then a very famous film star, so popular from
all the Road films. She brought them in, but
people like me had to entertain them.

Dorothy Lamour worried me. She looked

lovely in films but she hadn't got a very good voice and I knew she would disappoint a lot of the audience. I said to Lew Grade, who came up to Glasgow to see how it went on, 'Have you seen where you've put me again? Second spot and then just in front of her.' He said, 'You do well anywhere.' I said, 'I bloody won't go well there tonight.' 'You're joking,' he said. 'I bet you do.' And I was annoyed, because I did.

The idea of going to Scotland and trying to get clever was right out, they would chop you down. If you got clever, you'd had it. Jimmy Wheeler was physically sick for two weeks when they gave him a Glasgow Empire booking. I managed it by taking the mickey out of myself. And my bald head was my saviour. I used to take my hat off as I did my little song.

When I was just a little boy,
I asked my father,
What will I be?
Will I be handsome?
Will I be tall?
He said, No you'll be bald like me.

159

Then I'd have a go at them for laughing at my bald head. I did a lot of jokes against myself.

Frankie Laine was the best American star I ever worked with in Glasgow. The audience was absolutely howling for him, and I quickly realised I was going to have to do something really special to keep their attention. So I abandoned my prepared routine on the spot and just talked to them about Frankie's preparations behind the scenes. I did all this nonsense of shouting into the wings about him being ready, then at the end, I said it was an American tradition for the star not to come out until he heard the applause for the act that went before. I told them if they made enough noise they would see Frankie that much sooner, and it brought the house down. They went crackers.

The manager came round to see me afterwards and said that was fantastic. When I had walked out on stage, apparently all the stagehands just vanished. They thought I was really going to get the bird. I was alone on the stage and I just made the act up as I went along. I went out and said, 'I know you have heard me telling a few jokes tonight, but principally this week I am here as Mr Laine's dresser. Now he is a lovely man, just you wait until you see him come in the place, they are having a job getting him through the door . . .'

All the stagehands came back to the side of the stage when they heard this, and started listening like the audience because they weren't sure what was going on. And the orchestra conductor didn't know either. I leaned over and asked him for the chorus we had rehearsed that morning, just so it would look as though I had done something.

Frankie Laine was a smashing bloke. He came over on an enormous wave of popularity and yet there was no edge to him at all. Afterwards he came up to me and said, 'That was brilliant. What a piece of thinking that was.' I am lucky that I never dry up, and I can always improvise. I can think on my feet and the Glasgow Empire is the sort of place where you need that ability, otherwise you don't survive.

I had a thrill years later when Frankie Laine appeared on my 'This Is Your Life' and remembered my introduction so clearly. He really was a great bloke.

Lena Horne was rather more reserved than Frankie. She had a different attitude. I appeared with her at the Empire Theatre, Edinburgh. She was a beautiful singer and a very attractive lady, but she had her pianist and a coloured lady she called 'Mamma' with her, and no one else was allowed to get near to her. She was shepherded in and out of the dressing room as though you weren't there. I never bother with people like that.

David Whitfield went to the other extreme. He was a bit of a character, and he really was one for the ladies. I had worked with him in Blackpool and did a bomb because he brought in all these young people. Now I had to go on in front of him again, so I had to work up a bit of a routine about David as the girls used to come in their thousands to see him. I found inventing nonsense was the best policy. 'I bet you're all looking forward to seeing that lovely wavy hair of his, aren't you? Well, I've got news for you. His hair is dead straight; it's his head that's wavy.'

I got to know David well, and it was frightening, because he really was a lad for the girls. He had thousands of female fans and he seemed to get to know quite a lot of them, if you get my meaning. I was at the Winter Gardens in Blackpool for a summer season with him. He had number one and I had number three dressing room. We had Semprini between us, I remember.

One night there was a knock at my door and a rather attractive-looking girl stood there smiling. She said, 'David sent me.' I said, 'What for?' She said, 'Well, he's got a girl in there already. He said you would look after me.' I was shocked. I said, 'I beg your pardon. You'd better scoot because my wife will be here in the next ten minutes.

But that was just David. I counted them one night and David had six different women. No wonder he's dead. He looked twenty-five years older than me when he was forty. You can only go so far with that sort of behaviour. But he was a very attractive fellow. If he had had just a little bit more stage presence and acting ability he would have been a big film star. But they took him over to America and gave him a screen test and his appeal didn't work. It only worked with the girls.

He was a silly man really, David, he had a lovely wife. I couldn't do that to somebody I loved. Naturally men are men, they look round and notice other women, but with me that is as far as it goes.

I used to pull Lilian's leg. I used to point out handsome men and say to my wife, 'Look, there's a smart fellow. That is the sort of man you should have.' She would just say, 'I've got you, that's all I want. I don't want anybody else.' And she meant it, which was smashing.

She was always my greatest fan. She had a very promising career of her own of course, and early in our marriage she kept working. But then we had two lovely daughters, Anne Denise and Barbara, both within eighteen months of each other, and she preferred to concentrate on their upbringing.

I was away working at the Birmingham Hippodrome when Denise was born. Max Wall announced the arrival of my firstborn, in the middle of my act. He just walked out and stopped the show and said, 'Ladies and gentlemen. Bill has just become a father for the first time. He has got a lovely baby girl.' That brought much bigger applause than my act.

Then when Barbara came along I was away in Northern Ireland. I got this message saying 'Another baby girl' and I was so pleased I sent a telegram back which simply said, 'Thank you darling for Another Delight.' I walked across the road into a betting shop, and saw that there was a horse running called Another Delight – so of course I had a tenner on it. It came in at 20 to 1, so I won enough money to buy a new pram and all sorts of baby things.

We lived with Lilian's mother for quite a time and I was a very happy man rushing home from whatever theatre to be with all my womenfolk.

You need support in our business, and I

always got it. Some jobs are better than others, you see. I have this principle, if people come to see you, do your best. It is their privilege whether they laugh or not. If they did laugh it was a bonus, especially at the Glasgow Empire. That was such a hard place to be funny. I remember Jimmy James and his Gang getting off the train on a Monday morning, having a look round the place, and then coming up with the immortal verdict, 'It's been a long week.'

As I had taken Cissy William's advice about make up and so on, I was gratified when Moss Empires started to book me regularly. Without the paraphernalia of props I previously used, I pared my act down to basics and relied more on a sharp script than gimmicks. If Cissy liked your act she kept you working, and fortunately she liked me. She sent me off to the Finsbury Park Empire because she was in there every Monday night, first house. That was where they ran the rule over you. It was an audience full of agents who were tough nuts to amuse, I can tell you.

I used to take up the challenge. I would look out at them and say, 'I've got a new one tonight. You've never heard this joke before. So if any of your acts start using it, I'll know.'

I started as second spot comic, which is one of the hardest jobs in the theatre. You have two or three girls dancing for about seven minutes after the curtain goes up, and then you go on when the audience is still coming in, and nobody has come to see you. You have to go on and talk to them, so I had to work out how to get over that problem. I learned to work an arriving audience to such perfection that there were very few wanted to follow me.

It was Elsie and Doris Waters who got me out of that spot when they were at the Nottingham Empire with me. They had filled the place, but they were very gentle comediennes who had made a name for themselves on radio. I went on, bang-bang-bang with aggressive gags in a routine that really grabbed the audience.

There were roars from the audience and Elsie and Doris couldn't understand it because the show had only just started. They were immediately on the 'phone to London to Cissy Williams. 'We can't follow this man,' they said, 'he's too strong for us. You'll have to put him behind us.'

They weren't being rotten about it, they were being very truthful, so for the second house I was put behind them. And I never played second spot comic again. I did even better later in the evening because the audience was warmed up by then. So much so that the management of Moss Empires sent me back to Nottingham inside a month, which was unheard of. I said, 'I've only just been there.' They said, 'We know, but they want you back again, you went down so well.'

So I wrote a new script and rehearsed new songs – I thought I couldn't possibly give them the same stuff again so soon – and I went on and did the new act. I did all right, but not as well as before. The manager came rushing into my dressing room afterwards and said, 'What are you doing?' I didn't understand. He said, 'What they heard before, that's what they want to hear gain. You don't need to change a thing.' I thought, 'Oh my God, all that work I've put in was a waste of time.' I was inexperienced, but I was learning.

I have never been paid off, but I have had times when I've struggled. I never went down as badly as dear old Harry Secombe, though, when we were on two bills together at Huddersfield and Halifax. Harry was doing a shaving act which wasn't very funny. I advised him, 'Sing, Harry. You've got a good voice. Forget this shaving stuff because they're all funnier shaving in the morning than you will ever be.'

He took my word for it and he switched over to concentrate more on singing. If he hadn't they would have paid him off. They did it at Bolton Grand, one night and he'd gone. As an old friend and Army comrade I thought I was doing him a favour in saying something. I knew he had a voice.

The Bolton Grand was a tough place to play. I topped the bill there many, many times and I arrived one night to find to my astonishment, a huge cage containing two enormous brown bears. They had been working in the circus and some bright spark decided they should be on the bill with me. Well, when I saw these huge animals I was terrified.

I had the number one dressing room, which was right on the side of the stage. It was very small and I did a practice to make sure I could get out of the window just in case they got loose. It was a tight squeeze but I just got through. And I would have done, too, if those bears had come my way. They had the poor creatures' chains bolted to the floor of the stage with great big nuts and bolts.

But the bears had never been in a theatre before and as soon as the orchestra struck up they started heaving at their chains and trying to get away. The stage was going up and down and everyone started running for cover. They pulled the fire curtain down. They had the police in and they were made to take the bears out of the place. It was dangerous and they never did work in that show. I missed most of the excitement. I was hiding in my dressing room with chairs wedged behind my door. I was at the Bradford Alhambra as the comic on the bill with Henry Hall and his Band. The management objected to the song at the end of the act. It was a song I had broadcast dozens of times; a little thing that went:

It ain't gonna rain no more, no more
It ain't gonna rain no more.
If you see Cinderella with a fella'
Will you tell her,
That it ain't gonna rain no more.

I used to do little couplets like that, and:

Jack and Jill went up the hill,
Just like two cock linnets.
Jill came down with half a crown,
They hadn't been up two minutes.

They weren't having that here. This was a cathedral theatre in Bradford. So I had to go upstairs and send all my music down and change to a song I hadn't sung for a long time and do it with my ukulele. It was summer time, and I was that small on the bill you needed a magnifying glass to find me, and my dressing

171

room was so far up in the theatre I used to get altitude sickness. Up in my dressing room I opened the window and thought the church clock was playing my walk-on tune.

'Where have you been all the day, Billy Boy, Billy Boy.' That was my entrance music. In the distance I could hear a voice shouting 'Waddington', and I was trying to rehearse this new song. Eventually I realised someone was calling for me. 'What's the matter?' I asked. 'You're on!' they screamed from below. 'How am I doing?' I asked, like a fool, and made a bolt for the stairs with my ukulele. I raced down all the stairs, grabbed a chair to put my foot on, got the uke in position and just looked at the audience.

I was too out of breath to speak. I managed to get away with it somehow. I thought that would be my last Moss date, but it wasn't, because I told the office what they'd done. Lew Grade was my agent. He stood up for me and said, 'There's nothing wrong with that song. You've done it everywhere, Bill.' Of course they took notice of Lew.

My baldness never bothered me; I always used it for laughs whenever I could. When I got a chance for a top quality cover-up job, however, I was too intrigued to say no. Sergeant Stanley Hall, who was with me in Stars in Battledress, was an expert wig maker. His creations became very successful and he always told me,' After the war I'll make you a wig.'

He was as good as his word. He made me a wig and he only charged me £25. I thought I'd try it out somewhere I did well. I always like working Huddersfield and Halifax. In those days I would park the caravan between the two and have two weeks together, and it was one of my favourite bookings.

So I decided to give my new accessory a road test. You couldn't tell it was a wig. It was smashing. I said to Lilian, 'Go down to the front of the house, love, and see what it looks like.' I took my hat off in my act and carried on doing my gags as though I had always had a good head of hair. It didn't seem to go too badly, but she came up at the end of the show and said, 'Take it off. You've lost all your personality. It's not you any more.' I chucked it away. Well, I put it away in a drawer back home.

Lilian and I had a marvellous marriage. We used to laugh together and laugh at each other and it made life worth living. If we did have a cross word we would walk about the house avoiding each other, because we both knew the moment our eyes met we would be laughing and then we would both start apologising. Before you knew it we'd be having another squabble about whose fault it had been. We never had a serious row.

My career was going well and I was making some serious brass. Never one to hide my success away in a corner, I splashed out on the best car of them all, a Rolls Royce. I ran it for quite some time, then changed it for a James Young Sports Bentley.

My daughters were at boarding school in Derbyshire then and I used the change of car to play a trick on them. We were picking the girls up from school to take them for a cream tea in Chatsworth. When we came out of the school I pretended the Rolls had been stolen.

'Where's my car? I left it here,' I said. Then I whispered, 'If they've taken mine, we'll have this one. Jump in the back, quick,' and we all got into the Bentley. The girls crouched down on the back seat in case anyone saw them. We always had some laughs. I'll do anything for a gag.

Another time we were at Chatsworth having a picnic when suddenly we noticed a policeman behind a tree – then we saw another, and another. The place was crawling with coppers. We decided someone must have escaped, but we thought we were safe enough surrounded by all these coppers. We passed two coach loads of coppers, parked the Rolls and opened the boot to get the sandwiches out just as a big helicoper swooped over us.

The girls were waving up at it and the people in the helicopter waved back. It landed in the grounds and then took off again and everyone waved even more. We drove away and then read in the Sunday morning papers that it was John Kennedy who had been to visit his sister's grave. She had been married to one of the

Duke of Devonshire's family. If you have a Rolls everyone thinks you are somebody, even if you're not really.

We had been living in Leicester with Lilian's mother for quite a time, and this was very convenient, but I really wanted us to have a place of our own. We wanted a place in the country where I could rear animals and the girls would have space to play. I was working at the Manchester Palace while I was building our first home. I built a cottage in a village just outside Oldham. We were very excited about it, but even in those days you did have to have a building licence.

I was staying in a little hotel near Saddleworth. When I arrived they told me, 'We only have one room left, Mr Waddington, and something strange happens in it every night. We have a Great Dane and it loves that room, and every night it jumps at the door, bursts it open with its great weight and jumps on the bed. It has frightened so many people.'

I thought, if I know it's coming it won't get in. So I put a chair against the door knob, and

I heard the dog come bounding up but it couldn't get in and just went away. I thought, there's a story here somewhere. That night I was into my usual routine about lousy digs, and I added a bit about the landlady telling me her Nellie walks around in the night, don't forget your door; I said, no, I'll take it off the hinges. Half past one in the morning Nellie arrives and she's the biggest red setter I've seen in my life. I can't explain why, but Great Dane is not funny, red setter is. That's how a joke comes from real life. I was looking for fun in anything. I laugh inside all the time.

So I had bought this smallholding in Grotton, just outside my home town, but I was having terrible trouble getting permission to build. I planned to go into pigs in a big way, and since I was on the stage they wanted to know how much I knew about pig farming.

One Monday night I played at the Carrick Theatre, Southport, and that night I had a dream that they were putting up the walls of my new home and papering them as soon as they were up. I always wrote to my wife every day I was away and 'phoned her ever night. For the want of something interesting to put in my letter, I wrote about this dream in the letter Lilian received on the Wednesday morning. On the Tuesday I got a message from the wife of a cousin of mine telling me that I had got the licence to build my house.

My dream had come true. I sent off a telegram to Lilian saying precisely that and she knew exactly what I meant. It was fantastic. I built a cottage there for us, employing many good craftsmen, but overseeing the job myself. It cost me £3,500 and it was a marvellous place. I got into pig rearing there and I also had about 2000 turkeys. I was very busy, doing theatres at night and trying to fit in my farm work during the day, but hard work has never bothered me. It still doesn't.

Just after we moved in, I remember I was working down in Wales in Newport, near Cardiff. And all that week I had dreadful toothache. I was top of the bill so I couldn't go and have the tooth out in case it messed my act up. Every day that week I had been dousing this tooth in whisky, which was the only pleasure I had, and trying to get some sleep. I couldn't sleep at night.

On the Saturday morning I couldn't stand it any more. I thought, if I only miss one night it won't be too bad. I went to the dentist and he told me the tooth would have to come out. He gave me an injection and waited for it to take. But when he touched my tooth it still sent spasms of pain right through my body. He gave me another injection. But although I was going numb all over my tooth still had me in agony.

Eventually he pulled the tooth out, and the one next to it. The pain stopped. That night after the show I was very tired but I set off for my new home all the same. I drove for hours, until I was so tired I couldn't drive any more. So I pulled in to the side of the road and went to sleep slumped over the wheel of my car, a big old thirty-horsepower Ford.

When I woke it was daylight and I spotted a little hut with pushbikes outside it. There was a man in the hut, and I asked him for a cup of tea and said how enterprising it was of him to be up early on a Sunday morning. He looked at me as though I had got two heads. 'It's not morning, it's Sunday night nearly,' he says. 'Are you the bloke who has been asleep in that car all day?'

I panicked then and rushed off home which, once I had got my bearings, turned out to be all of a mile away. Lilian was so relieved to see me. She had had the police out and had been worried sick. What with the lack of sleep and the whisky and the anaesthetic it's a wonder I woke up before Wednesday.

I chose the village of Grotton because I could work fifty-two weeks of the year in a different theatre every week without having to live away from home. I loved to go home every night.

Once we had moved there, I used to tour the country, and at the weekend I couldn't get home fast enough. On Saturday nights I would drive through the night to get home, and if I told Lilian I'd be home at about half-past two she would be up waiting, all dressed up with full make up and everything to look her best. We would have a meal together and talk and laugh and enjoy our reunions. And if I arrived at twenty-five past two I would park up and wait at the end of the street to try to get there exactly at the right moment.

Sydney Grace was the man at the Grade office who looked after me and made sure I always kept working. He was, like Lew and Leslie, a very clever man. I only wish I had followed his advice. In the mid-fifties, when they were setting up the new independent television companies, he suggested to me that I put £500 into one of the companies.

At that time I was still working hard to put a home together, and £500 was worth a lot more then than it is now. I said, 'Well, I'll think about it.' By the time I had thought about it I would have needed £5,000 for the same investment. If I had done what he told me with £500 in the first place I would have been a millionaire without thinking about it. But that's hindsight.

Lew was always a tough guy to work for. He came up to see me once, when I was in summer season at Blackpool. I asked him whether it would be possible to organise a couple of weeks off for me to spend with my wife and daughters. 'What do you mean?' says Lew. 'You've just had six months in Blackpool.' He thought that was a holiday – working six nights a week in Blackpool and then going up for a Sunday night show in Morecambe. I was that busy the girls went to school in Blackpool for a while.

Clifford Davis, my old wartime colleague from the Blue Pencils, came up to Blackpool, when I was doing my first summer season. He got in touch and said he was doing an article about all the comics in the resort, but when it came out I was played right down and he raved about other comics who are long since forgotten. I knew he was trying to get his own back, but I didn't care. I went on to do the Royal Command Performance while his tips for the future faded into obscurity.

Lilian was getting a bit fed-up with me working all the time, so I booked her and the girls in to see a show called *A Kid for Two Farthings*, a real weepy, all about a unicorn. I arranged to pick them up when it was over, and when I arrived my wife came out and I saw she had been crying. But I could tell she'd been crying with laughter.

'Oh!' she said, 'What a night!' When the man came on to steal the unicorn, Denise, who was above five then, jumped up at the crucial quiet moment and shouted, 'Waken up, you dozy bugger, he's stealing your bloody nanny goat!' It brought the place down. She had heard the fellows on the farm swearing, and that came out.

The fifties were fantastic for me. I had a growing family to support and happily the work kept pouring in. The feeling of exhilaration in front of a laughing audience never wore off. And I also enjoyed a long success on the radio. I built on my wartime shows, 'Private Smith Entertains', 'Middle East Merry Go Round', and so on, and managed to move on

183

to make hundreds of appearances on shows like 'Workers' Playtime', 'Merry Go Round', 'London Lights', and many others.

But the highlight of my career was the Royal Variety Performance. The best thing about it was that it was held at the Royal Opera House, Blackpool, always one of my luckiest towns. It was the first time the show had been staged outside London. The Palladium was being renovated.

When they first announced the people who had been chosen for the line-up I was a little bit disappointed because I wasn't there. There were so many wonderful acts from America that there wasn't room. They were bringing Eddie Fisher across the Atlantic – he was the big singer of that time and they gave him a large slice of the bill.

That meant that some of the British acts were reduced in performing time, and many of them did not like it. Jack Hilton played merry hell about it, and Dave Morris actually refused to go on, he was so angry that Eddie Fisher had been given twenty minutes while he

184

had only seven.

I must have been first reserve, though; they called me up and were very nice about it, as though they had been going to ask me all along. I didn't feel so miffed about seven minutes. I just felt deeply honoured to be performing before the Queen. I said, 'I don't care what I do to get on the Royal Variety. I'll sell programmes, if you like.'

Around that time I had carried my lifelong affection for pigs into my stage act. I used to have a little piglet as a pet, who became part of one of my routines. I would walk along with him held in a shoulder strap, like a dog in a harness. I called him Pip, for Pig in Pantomime.

I was so looking forward to appearing. The line-up included George Formby, Frank Randle, Arthur Askey, Morecambe and Wise. What an occasion. But the powers that be wouldn't let me take my pig on. I wanted Pip with me, and it blew up into a big story at the time. Questions were asked in the House of Commons and the newspapers were full of it. A cat may look at a queen, they said. But what about a pig? I was planning to hire a Rolls Royce and a chauffeur, and the pig was going to arrive in style in a little crown and a purple jacket. It would have stolen the headlines, except that there was a newspaper strike at the crucial time. And the authorities ruled that Pip couldn't appear because he might make a mess on the stage. I said, 'How can it make a mess if I don't feed it?'

I have met some marvellous people in show-business but one of my favourites was dear old Sidney James. I was on stage with Sid at the Sunderland Empire the night he died. It was such a shock and a horrible experience yet when I remember Sid I can't help smiling, because he was that sort of bloke.

We were together in a farce called *The Mating Season*. He was the star thanks to his success on television but when I joined him and started getting a few laughs, he was more than generous. I might not have been a trained actor but I knew how to work an audience. I started putting in off-the-cuff lines and getting extra laughs. Sid loved that. He kept saying, 'Great. Keep it in.'

We became close friends and we were planning to tour with that show all over the world, but his tragic death put an end to our schemes. Bruce Forsyth took over the lead role after that and I did not get on nearly so well with him. Somehow the special magic of that play ended – for me at any rate – with Sid's death.

CHAPTER FIVE

Farm, Family & Four-Legged Friends

I HAD ALWAYS HAD A DREAM of owning my own farm. I wanted a place in the country where I could spend time with Lilian and my growing girls, a place I could always go back to, to escape from the madcap world of showbusiness and get back to basics. I wanted to breed pigs for part of my living, and I wanted to indulge my love of horses.

Not many people are lucky enough to make their dreams come true, but I managed it the day I bought the idyllic Weaver Bank Farm in Mitchell Vernon. It was our Shangri La. There was a magnificent old farmhouse, a huge range of farm buildings and 134 acres of the most fertile land. And it cost us £46,000, a superb home. One of the reception rooms had a dance floor. It really was a beautiful place.

It was all fitted out as the most modern dairy farm, but I wasn't interested in cows so I changed it and installed a brand new pig unit. It cost me an awful lot of money, what with automatic feeding and automatic cleaning machinery, but unfortunately it was not automatically money making. Pig prices often went down so low I was working like mad and still making a loss. I fed my pigs on corn and skimmed milk, no rubbish, but I never really made any money with them, however hard I tried.

Horses are such fine, noble animals; I have had a deep affection for them all my life. As a boy I used to go and work on a farm near our home in Oldham just to have a chance to ride a big old carthorse called Tommy. He was seventeen hands high and a great, gentle giant.

I would always ride bareback. I suppose I was thirteen when my headmaster saw me racing through the countryside without a saddle or a care in the world, and told me off quite severely for galloping on the hard surface. I said, 'It wasn't my fault, sir. He just took off.'

Tommy always did take off when I got on him. When he decided he was going home there wasn't much I could do about it. He knew exactly where he was going, I was just along for the ride. Ever since then I have always preferred to ride a horse bareback than with a saddle.

I think my love of horses comes from my mother's side of the family. Her uncle, who brought her up, was a very, very good judge of horseflesh. In those days, when they went to market they used to travel in a horse and trap, usually accompanied by a dog running underneath the axle.

Mother's uncle would go to the sales at Newmarket and buy a racehorse that had not quite measured up to running for a living but was nevertheless still a nice animal. So you never quite knew what you had between the shafts. Great-uncle Hague used to have a bet of five guineas with his neighbours as to who would get to the market first, and he nearly always won. He was a bit of a lad. My mother drove as well. She was a fine figure, clip-clopping around Oldham in her stylish rigout. So perhaps it was in the blood; horses were always important to me.

And I have always been lucky with horses. I remember, when I was about six or seven years old my father said, 'Right, you can have six-pence each way on the Lincoln Handicap.' I had been given a new pullover the previous Sunday, so I naturally chose to have my money on a horse called Pullover. It came in first at 66 to 1. That sort of luck has followed me all my life.

I love horses just for what they are, though. They give me great pleasure whether they win or lose. Horses are very noble animals; it would be a poorer world without them.

I owned my first racehorse even before we moved to Weaver Bank Farm. When we were still installed in our smallholding at Grotton, and my finances had improved a little, I was offered a nice animal for £250. It was called Sovereign Gale. I bought the amiable-looking creature, and I ran it in Lilian's name just to give her a bit of an interest. It did its best, poor animal, but it was never successful; a third at Doncaster was its greatest moment of glory. Lilian was never lucky at things like that, I was the fortunate one with horses.

The only time Lilian ever won anything was when I went to do a personal appearance for some old age pensioners while I was working at the Manchester Palace one Christmas. It was a pleasant do. They were running a raffle and I bought £5 worth of tickets. They asked Lilian to draw the winning tickets, and it was hilarious – there were twenty prizes, so she pulled out twenty tickets, and eighteen of them were hers!

The old folk were all shouting 'Fiddle!' and 'Fix!'. So I said, 'Well, ladies and gentlemen, that is the first time my wife has ever won anything. But we are going to give you all the prizes back, except for this bottle of whisky which we shall use to drink to your health tonight.'

Unfortunately Lilian's lucky streak began

and ended there; it did not extend to horses. I got a very experienced jockey to ride Sovereign Gale and give us his verdict. He climbed glumly off at the end of the trial and said, 'It's a lady.' I was puzzled. He explained, 'She's capable, but she just won't do it. She wants her own way.'

I was a bit upset about this because by this time I fancied having a winner. I changed my trainer and sent the horse to David Chapman, who still trains for me. We had Sovereign Gale tested and were told she had a heart murmur. She would be all right as long as she was not given any strenuous work, which seemed to rule out racing.

We took Sovereign Gale to Doncaster Sales, declared this sad diagnosis, and she made £125. The next time I heard anything about the horse was perhaps a year later, after I had moved to Weaver Bank Farm. I was taking a break from farm work to watch the racing on a Saturday afternoon, and I switched on to see the blasted horse win a four-mile chase, beating the favourite by twenty lengths. I didn't have a halfpenny on it and it was running at 25 to 1. I nearly put my foot through the screen. So much for her heart murmur.

But Sovereign Gale was a very unlucky horse. At a meeting soon afterwards she bolted and escaped, and finished up running over a road, and impaling herself on a fence and killing herself. It was a sad end.

I didn't really get into racehorses seriously until we were living at Weaver Bank Farm. It was a substantial farm, a very nice place indeed, my dream house. I sold all the dairy side off straight away, I didn't want anything to do with milking. I don't know anything about cows and I didn't want to learn. Pigs were my preference and, as I've said, we kept quite a lot of turkeys at Grotton.

When they did my 'This is Your Life', they told a story about a turkey that became a family pet because it flew up on to the roof and we couldn't get it down. I rang up the fire brigade to ask for their help, because I knew we would get some publicity that way and sell a few turkeys. The fire brigade came along, and with

195

them came the press, reporters from all the newspapers, asking what was going on.

As a result, we had so many people coming wanting to buy the turkey that jumped up on the roof that I could have sold it thirty times over even if it had cost £2 more! I made more money out of that one turkey than any other animal I've ever had. But they never mentioned my horses on the television programme, which was a big disappointment to me.

I may have known nothing about cows, but I did know something about pigs, and I wanted to build up that side. I refurbished the buildings so they could house over 2,000 pigs. I had 170 sows and the most modern automatic feeding and cleaning systems available. You pressed a switch and the feed arrived for the pigs. All the muck went into a slurry pit and a big tanker would come and spread it on the land.

But pig breeding, as I discovered to my considerable cost, is a very precarious business. It's either pennies or pounds. I tried to do it the very best way, there was no swill fed to the animals on my farm. But it's never just a steady living. And you can lose a lot of money, as I was to find out. At one time I was sending fifty to sixty pigs a week away to the bacon factory and losing £5 a pig. That was a lot of money and it was pushing me close to bankruptcy.

I was still working as a comic, doing theatres and radio and getting a few small television parts. But I wanted to have more time to spend with my family. And this had been a lifelong ambition, to have a farm of my own – I had always dreamed about a spread with horses and pigs. It was very hard work, but evidently that's something that does not do you any harm.

I had one man and two boys helping me. They all had to have their time off, so I found myself working long hours which I had to fit in with my showbusiness life. But I didn't mind. It gave me what I wanted, much more time at home with Lilian and the girls, who were growing up fast.

A lifetime of hard work has left me finding

it difficult to enjoy a holiday. I feel uneasy as soon as I stop. I'm wondering what is happening at home as soon as I go. I was looking back the other day and I realised I've had three holidays in twenty-four years.

My new set-up at Weaver Bank Farm was tailor-made for horses, of course. And the first horses to arrive were two stylish American pacers. They were fine horses, bred for the trotting races which are very popular in the United States. They belonged to a friend of mine who was short of a decent home for them and we went in together on the project.

They cost £1,000 each and when they arrived they were both in foal. I loved looking after these beautiful animals; the two mares foaled very close to each other. When the foals were about two months old we got a message from America that a two-year-old from one of these mares had just broken the world record over a mile.

All of a sudden the telephone got red-hot and the upshot of it was that we sold each foal for £750. We had a sequence of foals all of which we sold for a lot of money. It was only when life became a little more difficult on the farm that we sold the mares for £1,000 each. So we made a reasonable amount of money from those animals, and that got me going in horses again.

Weaver Bank Farm was a very interesting move for me. From my humble beginnings in Oldham I now found that I was in danger of becoming a fully paid-up member of the Cheshire set. The locals knew of my radio and theatre background and I think they were intrigued by my arrival among them. It was only natural that they wanted to take a closer look at us.

Our first move into society was not a huge success. Soon after we moved in we were asked to go to a whist drive in the village hall. There must have been 300 people there and at the start the organiser stood up and introduced me as someone they all knew very well from his radio exploits, and everyone clapped and gave me a very warm welcome.

It was mid-winter and very, very cold indeed.

They were playing cards in a long, corrugated-iron hut. There were two big braziers, one at either end, so if you were playing progressive whist, where you moved up a table for each game, you were pleased to get near one of these for a bit and get warm. Lilian was put on a different table from me. There was a real shortage of men, because most of the farmers had managed to find they had a cow calving or a pig farrowing, or some other decent excuse like an important meeting in the pub.

At the interval I was bang in the middle of the hut and with me were two old ladies, one playing gentleman, and a nice young lady playing opposite me. Then round came the buns and scones and cups of tea. I picked the stalest bun I have ever tasted in my life. It was like eating sawdust. I thought it must have been left over from the war.

I was taught never to eat and drink at the same time. But I couldn't help it, I took a big swig of tea to wash this dreadful bun down and got a mouthful of tea leaves. It produced a huge and uncontrollable cough all over this young woman in front of me. I looked up, and from her eyebrows to her waist she was covered in crumbs and tea leaves. She was wearing glasses, and she took them off and she looked like an owl.

Fortunately she was a good sport but one of the old ladies wasn't, she was in a terrible state about my appalling gaffe. I didn't mean any harm but I felt awful. Lilian was looking at me and I was wishing the floor would swallow me up. I had just exploded over the poor woman. It was one of the most embarrassing moments of my life.

Happily a much more promising introduction to local society soon followed. Our neighbour across the river, a successful farmer, invited us over for lunch one Sunday. He admired the pacers, then surprised me by saying that among his own horses he owned a half-sister to Arkle.

Instantly I was interested. We went out to his stables to look at this magnificent creature. He said that she was getting on a bit then, I think she was fifteen. He had tried to breed from her but all her offspring were on the small side and none ever showed any trace of the remarkable ability of her famous relation.

She had had twins twice. And really, as racing people know, you shouldn't let a mare have twins; they are usually very poor animals. He said, 'She always has colts. If she had a filly I would try to breed from her daughter.'

I've never been backward in coming forward and I heard myself saying, 'Look, I've got £25 in my pocket. I'll give you that if you let me have her for a breeding season and just see if I can do any better.' He smiled and agreed: 'I'd rather have her eating your grass than mine.'

He brought her round the following day. She was called Ancypancy. I had a good look at her and first off I did the first thing I did with any animal arriving at my place; I wormed her. Even if the owner said it had just been done, it didn't make any difference, I still wormed them. Then I started to study the book of sires.

Ancypancy's owner had told me that he had always taken her to very big stallions, to try to stop her having such small foals. But as that obviously had not worked, I thought I would just try something else. Heredity is a subtle business, I thought. I wonder if I can find a stallion which had a very big sire itself. Size can often miss a generation, was my hunch.

The biggest horse I could think of was Tudor Minstrel, which belonged to the Queen. He was an enormous animal; Gordon Richards, who used to ride him, used to say he had snow on his hat when he got off.

With my personal streak of good fortune working overtime I discovered that Tudor Minstrel did indeed have a son which, amazingly, lived just eight miles away from my farm. I would have gone anywhere in the country to find the right horse but, as I think you might have noticed, I've always been lucky.

I rang up the owner and said, 'You've got a horse there called Castlenik. Is he available as a stallion?' I was lucky again because this horse had been bought by a Japanese syndicate but the sale was not concluded because the vet had noticed that one of his testicles hadn't dropped. In spite of that his owner said he was in extremely good condition. He was a thoroughbred. And when I went for a look I was very impressed.

I was also impressed by the verdict from Timeform's Phil Bull who wrote: 'Genuine. Good ride for a boy.' They used to put a jockey on Castlenik at the start of the race and tell him to do nothing but stay on board until the end of the race and the horse would do the rest. He won seven races. So I paired him up with Ancypancy for another £25.

When she foaled she produced a filly, twice as big as anything else she had ever had in her life. I showed her to this farmer and he said, 'My God. Anything she has had before could walk underneath that, I'm not joking. And a filly as well. You lucky so-and-so.'

I said, 'Look, I am so pleased that I'll put her back with the same stallion and if she has a filly foal I'll give it to you. Poor Ancypancy would have had another filly, but she rolled in the field while she was pregnant and split her spleen. We found her dead. That is the other side of keeping horses.

But Nikancy, as I called the first horse I had bred, won her first hurdle race at an easy canter. This was fantastic for me. With horse-breeding, you can spend thousands of pounds and never see a winner. Nikancy went on to win or be placed eight or nine times for me; and she is twenty now, the brood mare of my flock. She has had a string of fillies and just one colt. That colt will never be sold. Her daughters are all marvellous, nicely behaved. I want to see what her son is like.

Lucy Lastic is one of her daughters. She has won a lot of races for me and is one of my favourites. Sadly her racing days are over now as she has injured her pelvis, but I am hoping she will breed and help to carry on the winning line. Breeding a winner is so satisfying. Anyone can *buy* a racehorse that wins, but to breed one is something much more.

Nikancy was the start of it all for me. I wanted to run her in Lilian's name but this time she said, 'Oh no, love. You're luckier than me. Register her in your name this time.'

I will never part with Nikancy – I always tell
her that when we part one of us will have died
– because she is the horse that started the fairy
tale for me. We are real pals now. I'll keep
working just to keep her, even if she never has
another foal. And Lucy I also have a great deal
of respect for. When her mother's breeding
days are over Lucy will take her place.

I began to build up a reputation for looking
after horses well down on my farm, and I
started to take in other people's 'resting' racehorses because they knew I would care for
them. I always prided myself that anything that
came to me went away better than it came, and
they all won again.

I got one poor little horse that was in a
shocking state when he came. He had been
overshod and had hardly any feet left; he was
in a realy bad condition. I rang up Newmarket
and got some top advice. I gave him a 'kill or
cure' worming dose, four times the normal
recommended one, and we got a bucket of
worms out of him. I bought special boots for
him to wear and his hooves gradually built up.

Then I gave him the regular doses of tender loving care that I prescribe for all my animals.

That horse underwent a total transformation. He became my pride and joy. He was first to the gate in the morning and he ran the place among the other horses. He became twice the horse he had been when he came, and I was so proud.

All the horses had different coloured head collars and every Saturday I used to take them all off and put them in the washing machine so the horses looked smart when the owners arrived to see them on a Sunday. Sometimes they looked so good their owners scarcely recognised them.

The secret was feeding them at the right time, feeding them in the proper way, proper worming, proper attention, out in the day, in at night. They weren't mollycoddled but they were looked after properly. At one time I was looking after fifteen horses all by myself. If you treat them right they respect you. They all have different personalities, quite different.

Horses are intelligent but they are not quite

as bright as donkeys. I still have my donkey, he's called Boo Boo. I got him one day when Barbara came home and said he had been badly treated. She wanted me to buy him to get him away from his misery, and as I'm a soft touch he cost me £35. The traditional wisdom is that you shouldn't have donkeys with horses because they spread lugworm, but I wormed Boo Boo properly and I've never had any problems.

Boo Boo is a great nursemaid. He always plays with the foals and looks after them. And if the horses were missing and had gone into another field you could bet your life he had bored a big hole in the fence and taken them all with him. But one shout and he would hee haw and bring all the horses home. He got fed at the same time as them.

Horses and good luck have followed my life. And it was Barbara who benefited when I actually won a horse in a raffle. As I've said our girls went away to a boarding school for a time – it was called St Elphin's, and was near Matlock in Derbyshire. We sent them there when I was very busy doing summer season and a lot of other work in Blackpool, and we wanted to make sure they got a good education.

But Barbara, particularly, was a very sensitive, intelligent girl and she wasn't happy about boarding. I think she thought we were rejecting her. We weren't, of course, I missed them both when they were away, but I wanted very much to do the best for them.

The school is near Chatsworth, the magnificent home of the Duke of Devonshire, and that was where Lilian and I would often take the girls for a picnic. We went there once to find the Rufford Hunt meeting and holding a charity raffle for a fine-looking hunter called Black Beauty. To cheer Barbara up I told her optimistically that I would win this beautiful creature for her for Christmas. I bought ten shillings' worth of tickets and promptly forgot about it.

To my delight and astonishment the telephone rang midway through October and on the other end was the secretary of the hunt. The old Waddington luck had worked again. I had won Black Beauty, or I could accept £250 in cash if I preferred. I dared not take the money because I knew how pleased Barbara would be.

I got Beauty, as we came to call her, back to the farm and could hardly wait for Christmas. I so much wanted to tell my daughter, but I love surprises – I just managed to keep it a secret.

Lilian's mother was living with us by then and I hid her present, a television set, in the stables as well. It was a freezing cold Christmas and I remember walking across the yard and doing a fandango slipping on the ice and struggling not to fall and smash this television set. Eventually the moment came and I said to Barbara, 'There is something else for you in the stable. Come and have a look.' I took her across.

When she saw Beauty, who had a sign saying 'Hello, Barbara' written on her bridle, she went mad with delight. She was captivated and spent all her time with this horse grooming and cleaning. She used to go off all day riding Beauty and worry us half to death.

But Barbara's hand in my horse acquisition didn't stop there. She came home from her riding school one day with a story that a Clydesdale mare called Corin was going to be put down because she had a bad foot. They wanted £100 for her. I hadn't seen the mare, but I said, 'All right, we'll have her.' She duly arrived, a lovely old carthorse, who reminded me of old Tommy. Her foot soon got better and Barbara loved to ride her. She used to hurtle round the field on this huge great horse but she could never get her to jump. Corin just used to stop and leave Barbara red-faced and fuming. I remember Lilian and I watching from the farmhouse window and roaring with laughter.

She was such a lovely horse we decided to get old Castlenik into action and give her a foal. Her first foal was a smashing animal. I sold it for £800, and I believe it eventually made £8000 as a hunter. It was a great big strapping horse with a bit of thoroughbred in it. In the end Corin had eight or nine foals and they all went well.

211

Our family had so many happy times together. Lilian was everything any man could ever want in a wife, because she was always my best friend as well as my wife. I think we had some of our happiest times at Weaver Bank Farm, when I had pulled back from some of my showbusiness work to have time to enjoy with her and the girls. We had such a marvellous marriage because we could laugh at everything together.

But from my lifelong efforts as a funster I know that comedy and tragedy are very closely linked. And so it was in my life. For just as I eased into blissful semi-retirement, and as my daughters moved into happy marriages and away from the nest, the worst tragedy of all hit us.

Lilian was struck with cancer. She fought it bravely for two years. We thought she had beaten it once, but it came back to strike the cruellest blow of my life. Lilian died in 1980, yet I feel that in some ways she is still with me. I feel she is watching my progress without her, and approving of my little successes. That I have become a household name again in the twilight of my long career delights her just as much as it does me, I know.

But her parting was agony itself. It was the most traumatic time of my life. I knew for two years that she was dying but I managed to keep the awful news from her until almost the end. She was a very beautiful woman and it was so grim to see what this terrible cancer did to her.

For a time we thought she had got over it. She had a hysterectomy. After that we went to see the specialist every month, then every three months, and then every six months and we thought she was in the clear. Then tragically all of a sudden it flared up again. I believe that had it happened today she could have been saved because the treatment has improved and developed since then.

My way of dealing with trouble is to work very hard. I threw myself into my work, I kept myself very very busy indeed. Towards the end my wife could hardly move about and she was losing her figure. And she had always had such a gorgeous figure. At first when she was ill I used to bath her and do everything for her, but in the end she was embarrassed and the girls did it.

I used to feel so hopeless and so helpless. Lilian used to say, 'I think it is over with me sitting about in the chair. Isn't it a pity that I'm going like this?' I would say, 'Oh well love, don't worry. It won't be long before you're over this and we'll go on a nice holiday,' not believing what I said for a minute, but saying it with all the sincerity I could muster.

I think I really learned to act then, rather than to be just a funnyman. Because I used to walk out of that room and go across to the stables and cry. I would kneel down and ask God to take her. I had never imagined there could be such utter desolation. I would do that and then I would go back into the house and make a big attempt to be as happy as a lad. I like to think I cheered her up. She did not know what was going on in my mind.

She died in Leighton Hospital, not far from Crewe and our farm. When I went to see her for the last time she was in a side ward, and she said quietly to me, 'I have come in here to die. I know now what you have known for a long time. God bless you for doing what you did to keep my spirits up. But please make me one promise. I am glad that it's me that's going and not you, because I know you can look after yourself, but don't start drinking, will you? Thank God it's me that's going, because I couldn't live without you, but you will manage without me.'

Those were the last words she spoke. She was dead in about three hours. She was a wonderful woman. I still find it hard to convey what she meant to me. We had thirty-two fantastic years together. Throughout our marriage she was everything a wife could ever be. I would just like to give two examples of Lilian. They are letters she wrote me, one deeply from the heart and one encouraging me before a big stage event.

I have already explained that, early on in our marriage, when work took me away from home a great deal, we corresponded every day and I telephoned every night. These two of her many letters remain my most prized possessions and perhaps show what a matchless

wife she was. On November 15, 1951, our
fourth wedding anniversary, she wrote:

> To my darling husband,
> Another gloriously happy year has
> passed and I want to thank you for it, my
> love, for every wonderful moment we
> have shared.
>
> Now we are four and a real little family.
> I have everything any women could want
> in life, thanks to you, pet, and God bless
> you always.
>
> May the coming years bring you all your
> desires, with your dreams and mine ful-
> filled. I could never express my feelings
> adequately, darling, but I want you to
> know how very, very much I love you and
> deeply appreciate your consistent kind-
> ness and help.
>
> I will love, respect and trust you forever,
> my own sweetheart, cherishing our deep
> love always. Again, pet, God bless you,
>
> Your own loving wife, Lilian.

Some time later she wrote some welcome words of encouragement.

Hello Pet,

Now relax. You will seem like a breath of spring after the tripe they offer so often. Play to Mam and me and the kids. Think of the false-teeth gag you did for us, it will make you laugh naturally.

You know and we all know there is nothing to beat on the programme, Reg Dixon is a has-been and he must know it! The secret of success is relaxation, pet. I know – I had to practise it a lot myself, to believe they really liked me, and were waiting just for me, and it does work. You don't need me to tell you that anyway. You're always good, so I look forward to seeing you – you handsome beast!

All my love, pet,

Your Lilian.

Now how could a man not do well in life with a wife like that to help him on his way? Whenever I walked into a place with Lilian on my arm I felt proud. She was a remarkable woman.

I am afraid that, after her death, I did not entirely follow Lilian's advice on drinking, though. I have never been a heavy drinker. But the trouble is that when you're alone you tend to drink more than you should, and alone in Weaver Bank Farm after Lilian died was the most difficult time of my life.

I had twenty brood mares at that time. I got rid of all the pigs, and I was looking after all the horses myself to keep myself fully occupied. I had no help, I didn't want it. My daughters were wonderful but they had their own lives to lead. I got very, very low at times. I remember one day one of the horses had kindly left a huge pile of manure in the yard and as I walked past it, I said, 'I'll be back to clean you up in a minute.'

Then I thought for a moment, and I had to laugh at myself. If I'm talking to horse manure, I reckoned, I must be going off my chump. In the evenings I would sit down with a bottle of whisky by my side and go over my life very quietly. Then I would get up the following morning and realise I had drunk half a bottle of whisky and I didn't really know I'd drunk it. I decided to knock that on the head. I only drink in strict moderation now and then I have two pints of water before I go to bed.

Lilian and I used to share everything. If I was cooking the lunch she would prepare the vegetables. I have always found that is the right thing to do, to share in life. And you have to share the bad things as well as the good. A pleasure shared is doubled and a trouble shared is halved, that's how I look at it.

I think if Lilian hadn't died I would have stayed on at the farm, I was so happy there. After years of missing out on so much of family life, with all the travelling around and staying away, I had my family round me and I loved it. I thought the world of her.

I have a photograph on my bedroom window and when I pull the curtains at night it's the last thing I see and when I open them in the morning, it's the first thing I see. But I'm not sanctimonious or silly about it, she's just there and I say, 'Hello, love' – and why not? If I get anxious about things, I talk to her in my mind and ask her, 'What do you think, love? Would you do this or that?' and it seems to help me to work things out.

It sounds daft I know, but I feel she is watching over me. I was looking for my car keys one morning and I couldn't find them anywhere. I had been through all my pockets, my drawers – everywhere – and finally I just looked at her photograph and said: 'Come on, love. I'm going to be late for an appointment. Where are they?' At that moment a pair of trousers dropped down in the wardrobe that I'd been through already and the keys dropped out of the pocket. It was uncanny and a bit frightening. Maybe it was a complete coincidence, but I don't think so.

Things have always happened in the most

peculiar way in my life. Just forty-eight hours before I was told I was going into Coronation Street I was talking to Lilian's photograph. I had been offered lots of little bits of theatre work and TV and radio parts, but I said to her, 'You know, love, I've really got to get something that keeps me going all the time. It's all right doing these odd things, it's helping me to keep the wolf from the door, but I still have to work all the time. You know me. I can't sit about.'

Life was never intended to be lived alone. Lilian is in my thoughs all the time in the nicest possible way. If someone has been with you all of those years and you have been totally compatible as we were, you want to keep them in your mind as much as possible. I feel very lucky to have had such a happy marriage; there is nothing better than a happy marriage and nothing worse than a bad one. If I wished anyone anything I would wish them a good partner.

Marriage is a great solace. I have wonderful memories of our life together, and if I had my time again I would love to start from scratch and do it all again for her. She was my reason for living, and she still is, because I know if there is any hereafter she will be pleased and proud of me.

One morning, when we were having a tough time down on the farm, Lilian said, 'I see your bank statement has come.' I tried to protect her from that sort of thing. I always thought one of us worrying was enough. She wasn't a well person by then, either, so that was another reason to try to shield her. She never knew what was in the statement; I just said, 'Yes, I've had a look. I think I'll have it published as a horror story.'

After Lilian died I stuck it out on the farm for another fourteen months, but the magic of the place went with her. It was much too big for one person anyway, but when Lilian went, part of me went too.

I was desperately lonely after she died and, still full of sorrow and remorse, I did meet another woman. We married very quickly, with me thinking this was the answer to my problems and swiftly finding out I was wrong. We both realised we had made a sad mistake and we ended the marriage. We stayed friends and still talk occasionally on the telephone, but it was just a sorry mistake for both of us.

Apart from Lilian I am not lucky with women. She was a great friend, a beautiful woman, a very straightforward person who never did anybody any harm; we had our troubles but we fought them together, and we never seriously fell out.

Of course Coronation Street has been an enormous help to me in facing up to my new life alone, but then so have my beloved horses. I have made bits of money here and there with my horses, but, much more important to me, I have had countless hours of pleasure and comfort from them, seeing these beautiful animals grow up. The breeding goes on, of course. And I am gradually getting better at it, because these days I am able to afford better stallions. I don't spend money just for the sake of spending it. I think about what I do. I am more careful these days.

I have had some difficult times, particularly when the farm was going badly, so I tend to be very careful with money. And I am very careful with my horses as well. I study the video tapes of my horses in races and if I see any jockey knocking them about too much then they don't ride for me any more, I don't care who they are. Horses never need hammering. Too much whip can sour the animal. Jockeys should use the whip more as a conductor's baton than as a punishment.

I have ten horses now and I love them all. I gave away one, Miss Plumes, to a fellow who has done me a lot of favours. She won eight races. The people I have met through racing are a delight as well. Most of them are country-men and I think they respect the fact that I have a deep interest in the horses. I'm not just doing it because of Coronation Street. I have been in the game for more than twenty years and I still love it.

I have always looked upon racing as some-thing to throw my energy into. I am not the sort of person who wants to take life easily, even at seventy-six. I don't want to sit and vegetate and stare at the wall. I love life too much.

I have still got the go-ahead to call a horse Coronation Street, but I am waiting for the right animal to come along. I have to be very careful about this, because it goes without saying that it has to be a winner. My last ambition is perhaps to have a day out at a big meeting, with a party of Coronation Street friends, watching a horse of mine called Coronation Street romp home by a mile in a big race. The show is a world beater so the horse will just have to be something equally special.

Index

Index

Finsbury Park 166
Glasgow 158, 159-61, 166
Nottingham 167-8
Sunderland 186
see also Moss Empires
ENSA 128
Epsom 137-8
Evangelists' Sunday School, Oldham 44

Ferrier, Arthur 116
Finsbury Park Empire 166
Fisher, Eddie 184
Folkestone 145-6
Formby, George 76, 83, 117, 185
Forsyth, Bruce 187
Freehold School, Werneth 49
French Fruit Growers 26-7

George and Dragon, Castleton 82, 83, 84, 87, 112
Gillingham, Dorset 95-106 *passim*
Gladys (childhood sweetheart) 51-2
Glasgow Empire 158, 159-61, 166
Grace, Sydney 181-2
Grade, Low and Leslie 157-8, 159, 172, 181-2
Grotton 177-8, 180, 192, 195

Hague, Epsie (mother) 35-53 *passim*, 60-68 *passim*, 76, 77, 82, 83, 86, 87, 91, 111-12, 192
Hague, Joseph (great uncle) 38, 78, 191-2
Halifax 169, 173
Hall, Henry 143, 171
Hall, Sergeant Stanley 173
Haynes, Arthur 124-5, 126, 134-5
Hertford 106
Hilton, Jack 184
Hollins High School 54, 56
Horne, Lena 158, 162
Howarth, Jack 17-18
Huddersfield 169, 173

Ingram, Inky 109

James, Jimmy 166
James, Sidney (Sid) 186-7
Jordan, Dougie 48, 98-9, 100
Jordan, Mrs 48

Kennedy, John 175
Kershaw, Harry 23
Keylock, Ronnie 109-10
Kid for Two Farthings, A 183
Knox, Barbara 20, 22

Lagey, Cyril 128-9
Laine, Frankie 160-62

Lamour, Dorothy 158-9
Laurel, Stan 149
Laye, Evelyn 107
Leicester 146, 147, 149, 176
Leighton Hospital 214
London Lights 184
Lucy Lastic (racehorse) 205, 206
Lummox, Mr 47

Manchester Abattoirs 64
Manchester Palace 176, 193
Mating Season, The 186-7
Merrick, Phil 107-8
Merry Go Round 184
Middle East Merrie Go Round 183
Miss Plumes (racehorse) 224
Morecambe 182
Morecambe and Wise 185
Morris, Dave 184
Mosley, Bryan 13, 22
Moss Empires 156, 166, 168
Mumming Birds, The 149
Murray, David 157
Mustard Pots, The 114
Myers, Frank 114

Nellie (Red Setter) 177
Newcastle on Tyne 149
Newell, Norman 150-52
New Faces 115
Newport 178
News of The World 84, 116
New Zealand Lamb competition 70-71
Nicholls, Sue 20
Nicholson, Brigadier General 109, 113
Nikancy (racehorse) 205-6
Norfolk Turkeys, The 114
Normandy 126-36
Normandy Veterans' Association 23
Nottingham Empire 167-8

Oldham 35, 44, 55-6, 176
Olivier, Sir Laurence 18
Onions, Miss 50

Paine, Tom 145
Patch, Wally 145
Percy Sugden Appreciation Societies 24
Pickles, Mr 50
Pip (pet piglet) 185-6
Podmore, Bill 28
Private Smith Entertains 183

Quinten, Chris 13

Randle, Frank 76, 185
Reading 143
Richards and Marks 157
Riscoe, Johnny 157

227

Index

Roache, William 21
Robinson, Mr and Mrs (foster parents) 46-7
Rochdale Motors 82-3
Rochdale Theatre 88
Royal Opera House, Blackpool 184
Royal Variety Performance 12, 76, 182, 184-6
Rufford Hunt, the 209

Saddleworth 176
St Elphin's School 208-9
Samuel French (Publishers) 115
Scots Guards 124
Secombe, Harry 169
Semprini 163
Seymour, George 149
Southport 177
Sovereign Gale (racehorse) 192-5
Squires, Dorothy 152
Stars in Battledress 23, 117, 124, 128, 173
Summers, Jill 19-20, 26
Sunderland Empire 186
Swift, George 53
Swindon 143, 144

Tab (wire-haired fox terrier) 97
Tarmey, Bill 13, 15, 20-21
'This is Your Life' 162, 195
Timeform 204
Tommy (carthorse) 190-91, 211
Tucker, Charlie 154, 155
Tudor Minstrel (racehorse) 203
Twig (Airedale dog) 46

Waddington, Anne Denise (daughter) 164-5, 174-5, 183, 197
Waddington, Barbara (daughter) 164-5, 174-5, 197, 208-11
Waddington, Bill, and Coronation Street 9-34; at school 40-43, 49-50; boxing ability 43, 100-101; early performances 44-5; learns to play violin 45-6; fostered out 46-7; house moves 48-9; early comedy writing 51; develops rheumatic fever 52-3; early woodworking abilities 54-5; as choirboy 55; as Boy Scout 56-9; plays bugle 56-7; works in mother's butcher shop 59-62, 63-7; studies suffer 62; leaves school 62; with Argenta Meat Company 68-71; learns to drive 72-5; works for Blackpool Co-op 77; as medical salesman 79-82; as car salesman 82-3; plays ukulele 83-4; on life in a pub 85-7; friends killed in flying accident 88-9; in the Army 91-139; in Dorset 95-106; first marriage 104-106; as a member of Blue Pencils 106-17; as member of Stars in Battledress 117-24; in France 126-36; in Brussels 136-7; in hospital at Epsom 137-8; demobilisation 139; meets and marries Lilian Day 141-9; stage career 141-3, 151-72; buys smallholding at Grotton 177-8, 180-81; gets into pig and turkey rearing 178, 190, 196-7; works for Lew and Leslie Grade 157-8, 159, 172, 181-2; Royal Variety Performance 182, 184-6; and Sid James's death 186-7; buys Weaver Bank Farm 189; and interest in horses 190-95, 198-9, 201-11, 224-5; 'This is Your Life' 195; moves into society 199-201; illness and death of Lilian 212-22; third marriage 222-3
Waddington, Connie (sister) 37, 39, 41
Waddington, Epsie, see Hague, Epsie
Waddington, Evelyn, see Case, Evelyn
Waddington, Lilian, see Day, Lilian
Waddington, Marie and Ida (twin sisters) 37
Waddington, William (father) 35-7, 39, 43, 73, 76, 84, 86, 87, 88-9, 111-12, 139
Wakes Club 86
Waterloo Street School 53
Waters, Elsie and Doris 167-8
Weaver Bank Farm, Mitchell Vernon 189-90, 195-9, 218
Wheeler, Jimmy 159
White Stone pub 87
Whitfield, David 162-4
Williams, Cissy 155, 166, 168
Winter Gardens, Blackpool 163
Wolverhampton 114
Workers' Playtime 184
Wynn, Anona 141-2

Zyal, Hymie 156, 157

228